The Timeless Storyteller

The
Timeless
Storyteller

Evelyn Francis Capel

Floris Books

First published by Temple Lodge Press 1975
Second edition 1995
This third edition published in 2014 by Floris Books, Edinburgh

British Library CIP data available
ISBN 978-178250-062-9
Printed CPI Group (UK) Ltd, Croydon

Contents

Note:
As well as lightly revising the language which has become dated, some of the introductory parts of the chapters have been slightly condensed. The text of the parables added into each chapter from the translation by Jon Madsen *(The New Testament,* Floris Books 2004), and any biblical quotes are also from this translation.

Prologue

'Tell me a story ...' It is one of the earliest pleas of children who are waking to consciousness. When they begin to tell their own tales, it is one of their earliest attempts to express their thoughts in words. From different parts of the world, myths are known today, telling of the world's beginning and the origins of human life on earth. They began far back in time when memory took the place of written records. Within each tribal group the stories were passed down from generation to generation. They began to be told as early as mankind had language in which to tell them. With the early myths came the folk-tales, speaking less about the gods and more about the first human efforts to live on earth. Ever since then, stories have been told and are still told, just as the child, having discovered the art of storytelling, continues to tell them all his life.

Tales have been told to convey the highest kind of wisdom. Plato put some of the greatest discourses on philosophy into the setting of stories about young Athenians meeting in the market-place, or at banquets. The Buddha told his followers many folk-tales of animals, people and gods to make plain to them his doctrine of compassion. Jesus Christ himself was a great storyteller. The Gospels of Matthew, Mark and Luke contain many short stories, called 'parables' today. Some of them were told to the crowds of people who gathered by the lakeside in Galilee. Others were told to the disciples and were meant particularly for them; still others to the opponents, including the clever and disdainful Pharisees and Sadducees. These stories were not a method of instruction for the simple-minded. They were that portion of Christ's teaching which he chose to put in the form of short stories. Even in modern times, when the intellect is so active that scarcely anyone has a simple mind, stories are a favourite means of communication. How many stories are told each day on television and radio, in books and newspapers? They are too many for most. We could be likened to children at bedtime who want one story after another, and cannot take them all to heart.

The stories of Jesus Christ are original to him. He composed them and told them himself. They are, one would say in modern terms, his copyright. They open his mind to those who listened at the first telling and to Bible-readers of every generation since then. They are stories about the storyteller, giving information about himself and his intentions. Such information was much required then, as it still is now, because the storyteller was not of this world and not easily understood here.

He came from the world of God, where he held the Son's place, to earth, where he had never before lived in human form and encountered men and women. He was a stranger in respect of earthly affairs and happenings. He was known only to those people who were well instructed in the things divine and who recognised in him the foremost of the Sons of God. All who met him needed an introduction. Those who awaited the promised god had to be reconciled to the human appearance. Those who saw merely the quiet human figure had to penetrate through the impression to find the god. There was no one to give the introduction but himself, no one but himself to explain how and why he had appeared on earth. He spoke comprehensively of his purpose through the parables.

They are the subject of the studies that follow here. They are made from the point of view of someone listening to stories, but as a modern person would listen. The original hearers did not listen in the same way as we would now. They were people of another age, that is to say with another mind or state of consciousness. History is often represented as a series of outer events, but it is just as much or more a long process of changes in people's consciousness. Thoughts and feelings were different in earlier times, as were outlooks and aims. The parables themselves transcend the variations of consciousness that have come about during the centuries of Christianity. They can open the mind of Christ to human minds at each state. But at each they should then be listened to afresh, for the ears that hear will be different. These stories were not told once and for all, a long time ago in the Holy Land. They are told for all generations of Christians and what they have to say will grow continually from age to age, from stage to stage of human consciousness. They will last as long as the human mind continues to think.

Today we understand what it means to 'do it yourself'. Our listening is in this vein. These studies represent the attempt of one listener – the author – to do it herself, but with two conditions. This listener could not have so listened without the ideas about Christianity which Rudolf Steiner brought into the modern world. Each person hears with the kind of mind which they bring to what they hear. The parables give of their best to those who bring such spiritual knowledge to meet them. The writer has found this to be so and readers can put it to the test for themselves. The second condition is that it should be conceded that the thoughts presented in these pages do not attempt to exhaust the subject, but are meant to stimulate all who read to listen themselves to the parables and to ponder on them in their own way. The intention is not to consume the meaning of the stories, but to kindle sparks in the mind that will set glowing other flames of understanding.

A certain method of listening to the parables has been followed which will be readily apparent in the studies themselves. Care is taken in the first place to observe as accurately as possible the picture in each parable. The listener can start by asking himself: what is the picture about, who are the characters contained in it?

Such a simple question can produce unexpected results. There is, for instance, a parable about a wedding in which neither the bride nor the bridegroom appear upon the scene (Matthew 22). How can this be? The listener does well to bear such a question in his mind patiently during his study of the story, without looking for an answer instantly. Great vistas of meaning can begin to open up behind such a scene when it is pondered longer.

The next question which is a useful guide to observation is: what details are included in the story and what is omitted? In one parable (Luke 15) the clue to the story as a whole is found in a ring. It is, in regard to reading all such stories, of great value to notice what has been left out and compare it with what has been included. The parables speak in a double language, through what is said and what is not said. When both are observed side by side they begin to yield up deeper meanings to the listener. This is not to suggest that each listener should fill in the gaps in the story out of his own imagining. More than once among the parables there is mention of an important person in the guise of a landlord, who has gone away leaving his estate to tenants. It is not useful to imagine all kinds of reasons why he has departed. But it is important to notice that he is absent, while still retaining his rights in the property, and to say to oneself: what is the difference between his absence and his presence? Is he active somewhere far away, although he seems at first to take a passive part?

A further question which the listener may ask is: what is said by the characters in the parable? Here again the distinction between what is said and what is not said can be observed. Almost all the parables are short by our standards but, in some, comparatively long speeches are made about a particular matter and all that otherwise might be quoted is omitted. Here again the question will prove more valuable than an answer decided upon hastily. Simple as these stories may appear at first sight, they are not so in reality. A contemplation of their deeper meaning may be arrived at through questions which the listener puts to himself and allows to rest unanswered for a time.

Another leading question is: what happens in the story, what is its drama? To follow step by step its events can lead to the finding of the clues on which the meaning depends. The parables are stories without any explanation included. They are presented in the style of a folk-tale, a series of pictures, characters and happenings without comment. In their style an absence of adjectives can be observed, except for those stating facts (for instance that a certain man was rich). It will be found that in storytelling adjectives are usually the means of introducing the emotional colouring that will affect the listener's reactions. In folk-tales they are sparsely used, while they abound in romantic literature. The style of the parables is bare but to the point. No listener will be led to taking sides among the characters by the manner in which they are described. Their words and actions will inform him who they are and he will find his sympathies for himself. Two parables are well known for having added to them explanations of their meaning given by Jesus Christ to the disciples at their request. But none contain explanations woven into the story. If the parables would be reviewed just as literature (an artificial but possible approach) they would be found to represent storytelling of the highest order.

A still further useful question which has been put in making these studies is: how does the story begin and how does it end? It will be found that most but not all of the parables contain a similar phrase: 'The kingdom of heaven is like'. The word parable means likeness. The story says itself that it is speaking in parallels, telling us what is like what. Each one tells of events that can be understood out of daily experience on earth. Who of the first listeners would not have seen often a sower sowing seed, even if it is more difficult to see such a thing today? Who would not have been asked to a wedding or helped with the harvest in a vineyard? Pictures taken from such experiences are called up in the parables as likenesses for spiritual events. The working of God in the world, in human affairs, is described in the language of life on earth. Nevertheless, the dramas happening in the stories do not repeat just what would happen among a group of ordinary people. The pictures change from the usual pattern because they are made transparent for the divine working. The pictures are taken from human life on earth; the drama is provided by God. Each parable tells the listener in its opening words that this is so.

The endings of the parables are almost always uncertain and unexpected. Some could well be said to have been left unfinished. By modern standards this might not be an artistic drawback but old folk-tales come mostly to a definite conclusion. A particular reason for the open endings of the parables appears from studying them. They are imaginative pictures speaking about what actually happens, about the history of man's existence on earth from the beginning on into the future. This is not yet finished; the outcome is still in the balance. The end is not predestined, although it is inspired with divine purpose. The parables are so true to life that they cannot have final conclusions, because mankind has not yet reached its conclusion. If they were inventions or allegories, they could be finished off, but they are, in the old-fashioned phrase, 'founded on fact'. They do not yield up their real meaning to those who read them without taking the pictures, with their details, seriously in a literal manner. Jesus Christ was a storyteller conveying highest truth in earthly language. His words were weighed as never before or since words have been weighted. They are divine revelations accurate to the smallest detail and deserve so to be heard.

It will be remarked that no reference has yet been made to problems of translation into modern English. This is so because today one can listen to a parable without encountering such problems to any great degree. Pictures described in so factual a manner as these do not depend much on translation. The true question is: what does the picture mean in itself? How is it, for instance, that the kingdom of heaven is like a king, or a father, or a landowner? Some historical information can nevertheless be valuable. Certain customs of the period are assumed. A prominent example is found in the story of the king who invited guests to the wedding of his son (Matthew 21). The guests were a mixed lot brought in from the streets on the spur of the moment. But one was dismissed outside because he was not properly dressed for the occasion. Today a listener might be worried by the thought that he could have been too poor to afford better clothing. At that time this problem would never suggest itself because a good host would clothe his guests with fine garments, which they would wear and leave behind on departure.

Another feature to be found in certain parables is the use of phrases taken not from the usage of everyday but from the sacred language of ancient ritual. Such a one is the sentence: 'For many are called but few are chosen'. It echoes back to a custom from the old procedure of initiation. The candidate was presented in the Temple and prepared for the sacred death-sleep under the guidance of the priests. If, in spite of the very real danger, he came rightly back into waking life he was filled with divine wisdom. He became an enlightened one with duties to perform towards those who were uninitiated. The phrase from the parables recalls the warning that many are called to take the path but few emerge to join the enlightened ones. Information about such phrases can be of great use.

The method of study on which the following chapters are based is a series of questions that the listener of today may ask himself as he reads the parables. They are the same for each story.

What does the picture contain?
Who are the characters?
What is said and what is omitted?
What words do the characters say?
What happens?
How does the parable begin and how does it end?

The parables are timeless and therefore meaningful at all stages of human consciousness. They are the means of God opening his mind to human beings through Christ. The pictures begin to come alive in our hearts; the drama continues to happen in ourselves.

The Story of the Sower

Of all the storytellers of earlier times the greatest was Jesus Christ himself. Open the first three gospels and there are the stories, composed by him, told by him, commonly called today the parables. The scene of the telling is clearly set out for each one. The storyteller is placed, the listeners described and the scenery pictured. To all outer appearance, it will have looked much the same when Jesus Christ spoke as when another storyteller began. In fact it was very different. Something happened in the spirit, for the heavens were opened. It was as if something was being born that had never been there before. Each parable had a birthplace and a birthday, chosen and prepared. The theme was there long before but it could not descend into picture and word until the right people were assembled to listen, the proper hour had come and the place had been found. This was not a matter of finding the right mood to fit the theme. It was a matter of finding the occasion when a new inspiration could enter human history.

The story, before it was told and heard on earth, had lived in the mind of God. It had been thought among his thoughts, had lived in his warmth of feeling. When Jesus of Nazareth, after the long preparation that made him into the most selfless of men, received the spirit of Christ into himself, the Son of God began to live, to speak and to be as a man. But the substance of what he said and did was of God. Every word and every deed was inspired from beyond the threshold separating the life of God from that of man. Each time there were the throes of a birth. What a struggle it is for anyone to express rightly in what he says and does the intention that was previously carried in the inner place of the heart. The greater the inspiration the harder the effort to find the expressions, the pictures, and even the gestures to fit the thoughts. Still greater, beyond comparison, was the struggle for what had been hidden in the mind of God to descend into words that could be spoken with a human voice and heard with human ears.

Luke 8:4–15

A great crowd went along, and there were ever more coming from the towns. Then he spoke to them in a parable: 'Once, a sower went out to sow the seed. And as he sowed, a portion of the seed fell on the path and was trodden on, and the birds of the sky ate it up. Another portion fell on the rock, and the sprouting green withered because it lacked moisture. Yet another portion fell in the midst of thorns which grew up with it and choked the sprouting seed. And lastly, a portion of the seed fell into good earth and grew and bore fruit, a hundredfold.' And with a loud voice he added: 'Whoever has ears to hear, let him hear!'

His disciples asked him what this parable might mean. And he said, 'You have the gift of being able to understand the mysteries of the Kingdom of God; but to the others they must be spoken of in pictures, for they see and yet do not see, and hear, although they do not understand with their thinking.

'And this is the meaning of the parable: The seed is the word of God. Those on the path are those who indeed hear the word, but from whose hearts the adversary powers take it away again, so that they shall not find salvation through the power of faith. Those on the rock are those who receive the word joyfully when they hear it, but then do not take root; for a while the power of the word lives in their hearts, but then, when other influences rise up, they go off on other

*ways. Those in the thorns, they are the ones who indeed
hear the word but in whom it is choked and prevented
from bearing fruit by their concern about earthly belongings
and by the cravings and wishes of earthly life. Those in the
good earth, they are the ones who receive the word with a
harmonious and good heart and keep it alive and patiently
tend it there until it bears fruit.'*

The three evangelists who record parables, Matthew, Mark and
Luke, each treat them a little differently. But they all agree that
the first of the parables to be told was the story of the sower and
the seed. True to their individual lines of approach, Matthew and
Mark describe first the scenery in which it was told and Luke
the human constellation. As readers of the Gospels we should
be badly off indeed without the variety in the accounts given
by the different evangelists. St Matthew (Chapter 13) and St
Mark (Chapter 4) tell of the lakeside where the crowds of people
who were seeking Jesus Christ found him at last. They had
come because they wanted something, perhaps without knowing
exactly what it was. In reality they were in need of healing in
body and soul. And they craved above all a sense of direction.
They were sheep looking for a shepherd. They did not come in
vain. They heard a story.

In their need, they pressed too hard and too closely. Jesus
Christ had to remove a distance off before he could speak to
them. This was so, both outwardly and inwardly. They could
not hear until they stopped demanding and he could not give
until they were quiet enough to listen. The crowds stayed on the
shore beside the lake and he went to sit in a boat, which could
be pushed out into the water. His voice came to them across its
surface on the clear air. The listeners were spiritually lost and
frightened people, but they could grasp what was told to them
in pictures. They were sensitive to the surroundings. They knew
that the world of water and air is not the same as that of dry land.
They saw Christ over the water, beyond the fringe of ordinary

life, in the place where they would have expected to find the old gods. In their time, and for long after, no one put to sea in a boat without offering a prayer and often a libation. The gods belonged also, it is true, to the land, the hills, the city and the household. But the water marked the beginning of the greater world beyond, where heaven and earth meet. For those people of an earlier time the clouds were heaven's doorway and the water the doorstep. They were awake to much that is not regarded any more today, to influences around them, interweaving, separating and alternating, to differences of condition.

They saw Jesus Christ in quite another perspective when he looked towards them over the water than when he was close by on the shore. Without the modern tendency to explain a situation, we should now say that they perceived at that moment that he had come from heaven, that he belonged beyond the water, the clouds and even the light of the sun and yet they could see and hear him. They stood on the shore, their homes, their fields and the dusty highways of the ordinary world behind them. They had come to the edge of life. They were shaken out of their usual concerns and emotions. The deeper spiritual longings were aroused. They looked out to the horizon, feeling the invitation to the soul to spread wings and take flight.

But between themselves and the horizon, answering their urge to escape, facing them where they stood, he sat wrapped in the light of the divine nimbus. With their old powers of sight, they were sensitive to such impressions, when roused. Emperors were still seen on occasions in a glamour that showed in a visible glow. Round Jesus Christ there shone a cloud of far greater brightness, reflected from the divine world itself. All that they had obscurely felt and yearned for was facing them in real truth as they looked towards him. They were seeing not dimly in a mirror, but face to face. They had come to ask and to pray and they were answered. The situation was so carefully constructed that they were not carried beyond themselves into ecstasy nor thrown into a mass emotion. They were left standing on the shore, their feet on the dry land of their own world. Their hearts were stilled by the surprise of seeing him on the background of the greater world, yet turning towards them, bringing them what they needed here on earth. And all the while he was directing them back into the state of mind in which they would not lose themselves.

St Luke has put the scene from another angle. He has seen Jesus Christ in the midst of the crowd but with a small circle of his own people round him. There were, he noted, the group of the twelve disciples and with them a following of women of uncertain number. The disciples had been especially called to follow him but the women came of themselves because, we read, they had been healed by Jesus Christ and were devoting themselves to him in gratitude. The other two evangelists have mentioned this following after the story had been told. Only Luke has started from this side of the picture and filled in the details. In contrast to the crowd of strangers who, in their excitement, did not know exactly what they had come for, a small group stood near to Jesus Christ of those who were bound to him by the tie between master and follower. He had become their whole life, the centre of their thought and feeling. The community between themselves and him had become so intense that when he spoke the thoughts and the words rang through their hearts as if they were their own, as if the group would think and speak together. No one can have remarked on this, for it was the custom for teachers and healers to move about with their disciples round them. It would have caused remark if he had come alone.

The presence of the followers of Jesus Christ was a vital part in the telling of the story. The crowd of listeners was there who wanted to hear. The situation was ready: the time and the place at the edge of the lake where water and land met. But helpers were needed, that out of the mind of God, through the mouth of Christ, the idea could descend into human words. The warmth of heart kindled by the sense of oneness in the community of those round Christ drew the story down into speech. Even in a more ordinary gathering today, one really interested listener can bring the speaker to life and draw his thoughts from him more effectively than he can produce them alone. Jesus Christ required human help on a higher level. He called upon the forces of heart in his followers to fashion the vessel of soul into which the parable could be received from the thinking of God, that it might be told as a story to the crowd.

After the telling, it turned out that the disciples were not, like the crowd of strangers from many cities, satisfied with the story. They expected something more. Going about with Jesus Christ, being continually engrossed with him, had woken up their minds. The people on the shore had been deeply affected by the picture of the One who spoke to them from the water. They had accepted the story into their hearts as the soil will receive a seed. But the disciples wanted more. They asked to understand what they had heard but they could not supply the interpretation for themselves. They asked and were answered with an explanation that appealed to their thinking. At the beginning of the story, they had helped by the way in which they listened. At the end, by asking a question, they helped to transform the picture into conscious understanding. From receiving an imaginative impression they advanced to grasp an inspired thought.

What did all these various people hear? They heard a story about something which they all had seen many times, about a man sowing seed. Nothing was said to them about what it is like in heaven, about what occupies angels and archangels. The story was about the earth and about a man doing a job proper to the spring. The parables all have this in common, that they speak about events well known in the daily life of the listeners. Did Christ then come from heaven to teach people about life on earth? He spoke in the language of earthly things because they are in fact reflections of heavenly ones. The earth itself was born at the Creation from the mind of God. His thinking has given shape to the things of nature and wisdom to their behaviour. The life of the earth can be justly compared to a book, in which

19

we can read about the thoughts of God. When Christ came into this world he could use what he saw around him in his stories because it was related by origin to his way of thinking. Nevertheless, the parables are not wholly derived from nature or human affairs. These have supplied the ingredients to form pictures for ideas new to this world, known earlier only to God himself. The parable of the sower is an example of this method. It begins with the sowing of seed, but the point that it makes would be useless to a farmer looking for the best crop. Only one quarter of the seed is said to have grown up to fruition. The starting point is simple but the conclusion is a puzzle.

Clearly the sower in the story behaves oddly. He casts the seed in all directions and does not watch to see where it falls. The ground does not seem to be his concern. He is only occupied with scattering. Three kinds of disaster befall the seed. Some falls not in prepared soil but in the rough land round the field. The birds take it all as their share. Some falls on rocky ground where the layer of soil is very thin. It sprouts but soon withers for lack of nourishment. Again other seed falls on untilled ground, where thorns and weeds choke the seedlings, after they have begun to unfold. A part of the seed is saved from these disasters, falling onto tilled ground with good conditions for growth. It bears a rich harvest, increasing a hundredfold. Why is the sower not more careful where he throws the seed? Why are there three types of disaster compared with one kind of success?

Such questions show that the meaning of the parable is not found within the scope of nature although the picture begins there. When the disciples, perceiving this, asked for an interpretation, they were told that the story is about 'the mysteries of the Kingdom of God' (Luke 8:10).

'The seed is the word of God.' But the word of God, the Logos, is said in the opening of St John's Gospel to be the one who created the world. The creating power of God poured out through the Word. In the parable of the sower Christ Jesus is speaking of himself. He is describing his coming to earth as an act of new creation, just as the sowing of a seed prepares for a plant that was not there before. The sowing of the word of God on earth is creation at a new stage. It is undertaken because the earth is without purpose unless a harvest grows and ripens. Once, at the first creation, man was brought forth as a creature within the created world. Now the situation has changed and human souls are to be in charge of part of the process of creation. The ground into which the seed falls is their inner life. The sower does not till the soil because that portion of the work is assigned to the people on earth. He brings the seed, sowing freely far and wide. The soil is provided in human hearts in every kind of condition, rough and untilled, stony and unfruitful, choked with weeds, or worked into good rich loam. The responsibility for the tilling is human. The risk is taken by the divine sower. The two are combined, responsibility and risk, for the sake of preparing the harvest. Man's history on earth has a purpose, so important to the sower that it is worth the risk.

The point of the story is expressed first in the picture perceived by the people in the crowd with the old kind of consciousness, in which seeing is believing. It is put a second time to the disciples in clear thought, which interprets what is seen before it is believed. Their hearts could know that God had begun the new creation by sending to earth the bearer of the divine Word, Christ, who was telling the story of himself. He was explaining why he had come and what would be their part in the great undertaking. He was showing them how necessary was their effort to the whole. God would give the divine seed but he would not till the earthly soil. He was giving them an insight into the way in which God views man's life on earth. His interest is in the harvest. In other words, he expects results. So highly does he value them that he is willing to sow new seed with all the risks involved, without which there could be no harvest. He expects not the largest quantity of corn from the seed but a particular quality of corn, which can be grown only in soil that an individual person has prepared in an 'honest and good heart'. He looks for quality, not quantity,

21

and therefore takes the risk of losing seed in unprepared soil. If quantity were the aim, then the sower would have to prevent the disasters by preparing the ground himself. Quality is the first consideration, and yet one seed of the right kind is capable of a high yield, even to a hundredfold.

What is the secret of the special quality that God expects? There is something which can only be cultivated on earth by human effort. It is freedom. It is of such value for the future that God himself has provided the divine seed. But it will not grow anywhere except on earth, for the necessary conditions are not found in the divine world. Separation from the constant presence of the divine is required. Only human souls between birth and death experience this state of separation. They are themselves often puzzled by their existence, suffering under its dangers and griefs, unaware of being involved in the great risk undertaken by God. Nevertheless they are called upon to make the essential contribution on which the harvest depends. God has put human beings into the position of meeting a world-need by what they make of their existence on earth. Separated from the divine world as they are here, human hearts can wonder if, after all, each one does not live for himself alone. It is a concern that must come with the sense of loneliness from God. Christ has recognised the human position and answered it with the stories told as parables. He has explained his purpose and that of the Father in the heavens to people on earth. The human soul is isolated indeed. But there is work to be done. The soil is to be tilled. The word of God is sown like seed. The harvest of freedom is to ripen.

The stories told by Jesus Christ are meant to be heard as if they were themselves seeds planted in the hearts of the listeners. They are preserved in the Gospels that they may be sown again from generation to generation. The crowd has never stopped gathering at the lakeside. Those who ask to understand more deeply are still coming to Christ with their questions. It lies in the nature of the stories themselves to live in human hearts. They have never been really finished. None of the parables has a proper ending. The drama is left open. There is more to come. No solution has been reached. In the story of the seed, questions remain, such as what finally becomes of the lost grains. Will the rough ground be tilled in the end? The picture of the fruitful seed opens up a still wider question. When the rich harvest, brought forth with patience, is gathered, what will become of it? Where and when will be the next sowing? Should any storyteller leave tales so little concluded? They must be so left, because it is the listeners themselves who will conclude them. Jesus Christ spoke of real happenings in human history. The endings cannot be told before they are made. They are not made even yet. We, the listeners, are the makers. Those who first heard the story of the seed at the lakeside must have known that it was told about themselves. Those who asked for the explanation must have perceived that they were being given a new responsibility. Jesus Christ is the storyteller whose stories are of the future, who continues them by giving them to us to finish. But it is he who never ceases to work in and through us, that we may in the course of earthly history be able to bring them to the right conclusion. Of such is the mystery of the kingdom of God, that the word of God speaks and creates in human life on earth to the end of time.

The Parables of Growth

The parables about the sowing and growing of the seed were told on the lakeside, on the shore where land and water met. A crowd of people had gathered there around the little circle of the disciples with the master in their midst. They came from their work and their affairs, in the quiet of their time off. They came sadly, for they had lost the meaning of life. They were 'sheep without a shepherd', their hearts heavy with the weight of a dead religion. Their minds dealt in pictures, using still the language of dreams known to their forefathers. Where the wind ruffled the water and the sunbeams brought sparkles of light dancing on the ripples, they could rest in daydreams from their cares and fears. But all at once there were pictures to see that were not only dreams but were of startling reality. The storyteller had begun by telling not one of the well-known tales but one that had not been heard before. It was new, yet it sounded like something long known and forgotten, as old as the foundation of the world and as true. No heart could continue in the old sad dream, when woken to imagination so powerfully. The moving air, the water and the dancing light became the curtain against which the pictures lived and moved through which the secrets of Creation began to be revealed. Absorbed and silent, they heard, saw and listened – a great ring of people overwhelmed by the answer to their deep, hopeless longing, the sheep who had heard the shepherd call in a voice that they could recognise.

The disciples were not so silent. Their minds had changed and although they too could escape out into the world of imagination out on the water they came more quickly back into themselves. They asked the storyteller for a meaning to the story after the manner of the dreamers of old who required interpretations. The faculty of understanding had awoken and they were not satisfied. This led to a change of scene. The consciousness of thought could not easily be maintained under the influences out of doors by the lake. The master led the questioners into the house, the storyteller became the teacher, the listeners the pupils. Their forces of mind drew inwards. They began to think, where they had previously dreamed. The head became the centre of consciousness. The soul of the dreamer is spread out over the world beyond himself. By contrast, the mind of the thinker is concentrated inwards, especially in his own head, and he contemplates the world from within. He is like someone sitting in a house, looking out of the windows, opening and shutting the door, but self-contained under his own roof. The body itself gives to a person the opportunity to withdraw and become a thinker. The hard skull provides his roof, the eyes and ears the windows, the mouth the door. While dreaming, the soul goes out of the house. While thinking the soul goes home again to itself. In the stories told in the gospels, a harmony is found between outer event and inner meaning, which is so often missing in ordinary life today. The setting and the happening coincide exactly.

Matthew 13:24–43

And he placed another picture before them: 'The kingdom of the heavens can be compared with a man who sowed good seed in his field; but while everyone was asleep his enemy came and sowed weeds among the wheat and went away again. Now when the plants sprouted and bore fruit, then the weeds also appeared. Then the servants of the master of the house came to him and said, "Master, did you not sow good seed in your field? So where do the weeds come from?" He answered, "A man who is our enemy has done this." Then the servants said, "If you want us to, we will go and gather the weeds." He said, "Do not do that, otherwise when you gather the weeds you will tear up the wheat also. Let both grow until the harvest. And when harvest time has come, I will say to the reapers: Gather the weeds first and bind them in bundles to be burnt, but gather the wheat into my barn".'

Again he placed another picture before them: 'The kingdom of the heavens is like a grain of mustard which a man takes and plants in his field. It is the smallest of all seeds, but when it grows it is soon taller than the herbs and becomes a tree in whose branches the birds of the air build their nests.'

And he told them another parable: 'The kingdom of the heavens is like leaven which a woman took and mixed with three measures of flour until all the flour was leavened.'

Jesus spoke to the people in parables in this way, and he spoke to them only in parables. The word of the prophet was to be fulfilled:

In pictures will I speak,
so that I can uncover everything
which has been hidden
since the foundation of the earth.'

And he dismissed the crowd and went into the house. And his disciples came to him and said, 'Explain to us the parable of the weeds in the field.' He answered, 'He who sowed the good seed is the Son of Man. The field is mankind. The good seeds are the sons of the kingdom. The weeds are the sons of the evil power, and the enemy who sowed the weed is the Tempter himself. The harvest is the completion of the cycle of time, and the reapers are the angels. Just as the weed is gathered and burnt in the fire, so will it be at the completion of the cycle of time. The Son of Man will

send out the angels who serve him, and out of his kingdom
they will gather all obstacles to the true self and all those who
are in the service of anarchy and chaos, and hand them over
to the world fire.
  'Those concerned must endure an existence of lamentation
and gnashing of teeth. But those who serve the Good will
shine like the sun in the kingdom of their Father. He who
has ears, let him hear!'

So it is with the parables of growth as they are told in the Gospel
of St Matthew, Chapter 13. As well as the parable of the sower,
three other stories were told beside the lake. The disciples asked
for an interpretation. In response to their request to understand,
Christ led them from the shore into the house, from the world
outside to the inner place of the soul within the body.

The four stories have one thing in common – they speak on
the theme of growth. The first tells how seed was sown which
sprouted and grew according to the kind of soil on which it fell.
The next is about the weeds, which were found growing among
the wheat. The third is about a very small seed developing into
a large tree. The fourth tells of the power of a small quantity of
leaven to raise a great lump of dough.

The listeners must all have known what was described but
they must never have recognised with understanding what they
knew. They realised themselves to be living in a world of matter
working with things and handling materials. They had watched
what happened when under such circumstances growth began.
All that applied to the nature of material substance was then
contradicted. What was sown into the ground was living seed,
not deriving its life from matter, but carrying its forces into
matter. Life is not from the earth but from water, air and warmth,
which weave around and into it from the heights and the widths
above. When life meets substance there is growth. What comes
from above imbues what exists from below with its life-giving
influence, changing substance through a process that comes

from beyond itself. When the natural drama of growth is realised, it is understood to be the sign of the spirit at work in matter, of spiritual powers expressing themselves in earthly activity.

Growth is the drama of spirit and matter, of life and death encountering each other. When a seed sprouts, the forces of the sun, the moon and the earth meet from different directions, working upon one another. The earthly substance in the seed has to be impregnated by that which comes from beyond the earth. Sprouting begins, and the seed changes entirely into a new form. Again the old form disappears and a new one is produced. At each point of growth something new enters the substance. In a series of changes, new forms appear one after the other until the plant has completed itself. The onlooker watches the plant-substance seized again and again by a forming influence that seems to dissolve what is there and re-form it according to an invisible pattern. The process is that of something taken hold of from outside and fashioned into something new. At every stage there is danger. The forming influence may be defeated. The substance may fail to change. The seedling may wither before it has been completely transformed into the final pattern. The seed is the focus-point of a drama which may or may not be played out to the end.

The process through which a seed grows and a grown plant withers can be the subject of an exercise of the mind. When the seed is observed, nothing is to be seen with the outer eye of what it will become. The mind builds up the picture of the growing process which is not yet visible. When the grown plant begins to fade, the leaves, stem and flower lose their shape and colour. The pattern which was made visible by the process of growth disappears to the outer eye and is to be followed in thought by the inner eye. On the outside what is left over is the seed, which is quite unlike the finished plant. Seed and plant can be related in thought by the exercise of insight, but to outer observation they are quite different.

When the whole drama of growing and withering, of sprouting

seed and fading flower is thought through in meditation, the soul finds itself standing at the threshold between heaven and earth. The descent of the forming influence into the substance is felt. The forming influence can be observed changing the substance into its own image, reforming the substance to a new pattern. The forming influence can be seen to leave the substance as the plant withers, and to withdraw whence it came. The observer can have the experience of watching a ladder on which the forming influences descend and ascend again. The picture becomes more vividly true when it is transformed into that of a spiral staircase of moving light. The plant-forms move down and up the spirals, coming and going between the visible world and the invisible. At the bottom of the golden steps is the place where the substance exists which can be transformed into root, stem, leaf, flower and seed. At the top are the spheres of sun, moon and stars from which the original patterns of the plants flow down on the forces of life.

When, after dwelling on this inner picture, the mind follows the outer eye into the world of nature, its reality is confirmed by a particular observation. Any plant, in the garden or under the hedge, grows upwards with a spiral movement. If a plant is observed by looking down on it from above, the arrangement of the leaves will be seen in spirals, which vary with each kind of plant. Growing things go spiralling upwards, drawn by the influence of the invisible ladder between the two worlds above and below.

Such considerations can show how true to life are the parables in which the processes of growing in nature are pictures for what happens in the living evolution of mankind. The theme of the parables told by the lakeside is human history. The listeners knew from experience what happens each year in nature. What the parables had to tell them was the fact, which they had not realised, that human history is a growing process of a like kind. In a vision of thought, they could see, if they would, that the creation of man was like the sowing of a seed, which had germinated, sprouted and grown but in later times had become a sickly, withering plant. What was to follow? A bad harvest, a bonfire of the world's rubbish, a last judgment to sort out the little good wheat from much chaff? John the Baptist, when he prophesied the Messiah's immediate coming, spoke in such pictures. Jesus Christ when he came brought a different picture, the sowing of new seed into the old ground.

The parables, as they are related in the gospels of Matthew, Mark and Luke, are not the same throughout, but each evangelist opens the series of parables with the same one, the sower going forth to sow new seed. Those who met Jesus Christ would have already heard of his herald John or have seen him. They would have heard what he preached, 'He who comes after me ... will baptise you with the Holy Spirit and with fire. The winnowing fork is in his hand, and he will cleanse his grain of the chaff. He will gather the wheat into the barn, but the chaff he will burn with an unquenchable fire' (Matt.3:11f). Then came Jesus Christ and began by saying, 'A sower went out to sow.'

When he spoke of the new seed, of a beginning again in human history, he was saying nothing to contradict John's picture of the world-harvest. He himself used it on occasions, but at a later time, after the new seed would have grown and ripened. A grave question must have moved in the hearts of the listeners, as it still moves today in the hearts of those who understand the meaning of history in a Christian sense. Man had become by then, and still is, a spoilt being. Human history had not produced a right harvest. There was as much to distress the heart in human affairs as there is today in the news that pours in on us from all directions of the world. Was human evolution worth continuing? Is it still worth it now? Why sow new divine seed where so much has already failed?

The first two parables speak boldly to this question. Of the seed scattered by the sower only one portion out of four is said to grow up and bear fruit, while in three different ways the rest fails. The sower knows how to take failure with success, the bad with the good. The next picture contains the clue to the failure. 'While everyone was asleep his enemy came and sowed weeds among the wheat and went away again' (Matt.13:25).The sower has not the situation entirely in his own hands. The enemy is around. In Genesis, the First Book of Moses, it is said that the enemy appeared soon after the creation of the world and interfered with the seed, which was the newly created man himself. When Jesus Christ spoke of the new sowing. He described the enemy coming again. Why was he not seized and thrown out by the sower? But in the parable he is said to have warned the servants who wanted to be rid of the enemy's influence, 'When you gather the weeds you will tear up the wheat also.' The weeds were to stay, the enemy was to be left to come and go.

Enemy action is to be reckoned with as a fact in history, the parable would seem to say. The influences of evil are part of our human life. God tolerates them and Christ did not set out to destroy them. It seems to be essential to the growing and ripening of man's true being that he should be faced with the constant companionship of evil. Human beings are in the process of evolution, still growing because they are not yet finished products. But they are in danger throughout the time of their growth from the destructive forces that work around and upon them. All living things are exposed to dangers. Every crop of apples on a tree is harvested in spite of the threat of ill-timed frost, too much or too little rain, blight, insects and diseases. But the threat to man is of a moral nature and comes from within. The living things of nature are attacked from outside. Human beings are more deeply involved because, with the beings of evil as companions, they can will to destroy themselves. Human beings are not protected by the innocence that is essential to the plants and even, in a sense, to the animals. They are temptable. The enemy is within the gates. The decision between good and evil lies with humans themselves.

Man would never have come into such a situation without the presence of the enemy. Human beings would have been protected by unthinking innocence. As it is they must develop discrimination. They can make mistakes. But they can learn by experience, change, and start again. As long as there is breath in their body, they can turn in another direction. They can make or mar their relation to another person or to themselves. Being unprotected, they have become independent. As long as the weeds can grow in the field, it is a sign that the wheat has been sown in a place where the divine powers allow the enemy some scope. That is to say, they have withdrawn from the field which is said by Christ himself in his interpretation of the parable to represent this world. They no longer exercise control, for which reason the enemy, who is the devil, has access. Furthermore, the Son of Man sows the good seed there, knowing full well that the devil can and will interfere. Man has been put in the place of independence to evolve where the devil is active.

Man is in great danger. But his independence is God-willed; God has taken a risk with man, whom he has created. Christ has confirmed the risk by sharing it himself, when he came into this world to sow the new seed. What could be the meaning of taking so severe a risk with a being so helpless as man? Here, on the topmost level of history, the simplest of questions arises: how and why did God let it happen? Why does he not confound the powers of evil?

It is not the divine answer to the enemy, the original source of man's danger, to smite him. Instead there is another answer contained in the two short parables that follow those of the seed-sowing. The one speaks of the mighty force within the smallest seed to grow into a great plant. The other points to the influence of the small amount of leaven or raising agent to transform the dough. In olden times leaven consisted of a lump of old dough, saved until it was in a high state of fermentation, being inserted into the mass of fresh flour. The process working in the old dough was so active that raw meal was changed into bread. These two pictures stress the contrast between the outer appearance of smallness and the vital energy within. The good seed and the good leaven are so powerful in the vitality of their goodness that they can prevail against the hindrances around them. In other words, God has such faith in the good seed that is sown in and with man that he can take the risk of withdrawing the divine protection and leaving him to his dangerous independence. The danger is not prevented. It is answered by the living power in the seed. Man, when he sees the danger that he is in, may long for protection against the enemy. But the divine answer is found by looking in the other direction, inwards, to the living power of the good, which has been planted in man.

Why is independence of such importance that man has for its sake to live and grow in the dangerous presence of evil? It is not an end in itself, neither is evil. Both are a means to an end. The powers of evil have interfered in man's evolution at a time far away and long ago. They were allowed to do so, they have been tolerated ever since, but furthermore they have been used. From the human angle on evolution, they have constituted a menace. From the other side, from the divine, they have been used to produce an opportunity. The divine mind carries a purpose almost out of human sight, of such proportions that evil can be conceived as having a subsidiary part in the whole. It is a necessary part but only in the sense of contributing conditions that cannot be produced by other means. The power of the divine pervaded all creation at the beginning. Only through the strength of a will operating against the will of God could the creation fall away from the order of the universe and become a God-forsaken place, where everything is possible that is not divinely intended. The influence of the will against, that is to say evil, was necessary to produce independence.

In the parable of the weeds among the wheat, it is said that the enemy came to sow his seed in the dark, when the servants were asleep. They were unaware of his activities, so that they could not protect themselves. The owner was aware but did not protect either the servants or the seed. The enemy brought about conditions that shocked the servants into a sense of danger and the desire to act. Having to accept the presence of the weeds all through the time of growth, their sense of responsibility was constantly wakened and stimulated. The good seed meanwhile had to grow under opposition. It had to become as strong and stronger than the weeds. It would develop thereby the quality that is also known among plants in nature, which savours of the struggle for the near-impossible. The good seed was obliged to rely on its own vitality. Left unprotected, it could only thrive out of its own strength.

Independence is the opportunity to develop freedom. The mysterious force which can, in terms of evolution, be called free, lives within the being of man. He can discover it only when he is obliged to rely on what is within, becoming independent of influences from without. There is a state of innocence, in which indeed every human soul enters upon his life on earth, which makes what is good seem right and natural. It is God-given, being the after-effect of the soul's existence before birth in the world where the divine will prevails without let or hindrance. There is love of the good quite different in quality, which comes alive in the soul when loss of innocence, guilt, wrong and pain have been experienced. The love of the good of the first kind is accepted from without. The soul enjoys an untroubled sense of living with what is right. The other experience, in which the good is known and loved from within, is part of the soul's innermost being. It is cherished as something precious that must never be lost. It grows into an urge of will. The soul, loving freely the good, wants to share in creating its substance. Aware that the enemy is always at hand in opposition, the soul has to strengthen all its forces, resisting the menace from without, and calling up the spirit from within, to triumph in creating what is of the good. We know good of two kinds. There is that which stems from the world's beginning and is the substance of God's being. Likewise there is that which will have been created at the world's ending. That good will contain the creative effort of man.

The good is of the nature of light. But evil is dark. The good builds and creates. But evil destroys. The good kindles the spark of joy, but evil brings distress and pain. The good is worthy of man, but evil makes him into a demon. The good brings into the world that which is of value, but evil produces false imitations. The good builds, but evil tears down. The good will endure to the end, but evil will be one with the stream of destruction. When man, prompted only by the spirit within himself, works to create the good, he builds the new world that should arise at the end of his evolution. In freedom he creates within the creating of God, he becomes a creator in the service of the world's good.

When the stories of the seed and its growth were first told, the crowd heard them in a dream and the apostles with the intellect as it first began to awaken. Today they should be heard with the waking powers of the heart. They require to be understood with imaginative thinking, in which the forces of head and heart work together. The dreamers of old received the pictures as messages from outside and the interpretation from human intelligence within. Today we begin with attempting to understand and, pondering, we bring the picture to life in imagination. It comes alive individually for each person. As it comes alive, it begins to grow. New meanings appear from time to time. New feelings are drawn in. The picture has developed whenever we return to look. It is as if the mind of Christ, from which the picture first came, would live continually in it, renewing and repainting it before our inner eyes. It remains timeless throughout the centuries, because it is remade for each generation of Christian people. The parables that speak of the divine sower grow themselves, for they are seeds sown in human hearts.

In the gospels we read of the mystery performed by Christ when he fed the crowd of hungry people who followed him. It is described as an event of small beginnings in the physical life and of immense effect in the spiritual. A very small contribution of loaves and fishes was made from the crowd. As Christ gave thanks and blessed the offering, a flow of spiritual forces began to come from the universe into the inner being of the people gathered together. They were all nourished and fed. In the final details of the scene, it is said that twelve baskets of remains were collected for the future. The nourishment of human souls continues on through the centuries, dispensed from the full baskets. The parables are in reality part of what they contain. The life-giving gifts of Christ have been given again and again from then until now.

Parables of the Harvest

Everyone leads a double life by being both a sleeper and a waker. In sleep we are unconscious but grow wiser. Awake we are more conscious and have the use of our own will. During the waking hours we are alive and ourselves. In sleep we do not seem to belong to ourselves. We waken to become the centre of our world. Here are the circumstances which we can dominate with our own will, where we can achieve our own ends. The world that is entered through sleep is God-centred, but the world that is found on waking is mankind-centred. The two are separate. The human soul goes backwards and forwards between them, finding and losing itself, using itself up and being renewed.

Matthew 13:44–52

'The kingdom of the heavens is like a treasure hidden in a field. A man found it and hid it and went, full of joy, to sell everything that he owned in order to acquire the field.

'The kingdom of the heavens is also like a merchant in search of fine pearls. And when he found a particularly valuable pearl, he sold all his goods and bought the pearl.

'Lastly, the kingdom of the heavens is like a net which was cast into the sea and all kinds of fish were caught in it. When it was full, the fishermen drew it ashore and sat down around it and gathered the good fish into containers, but the useless ones they threw out. So it will be at the completion of

the cycle of time. The angels will go forth to separate out all those who have given themselves over to evil from those who bear the Good within them. They will be handed over to the world fire and must endure an existence of lamentation and gnashing of teeth.

'Have you understood all this?' They answered, 'Yes.' And he said, 'Every student of the scriptures who has been taught by the kingdom of the heavens itself is like a man who is master of his house and knows when to bring out what is new and when what is old from his treasures.'

In the previous chapter we saw the world which is man's is the field of which the parables speak. Here the seed has been sown, the weeds have grown beside it and the harvest will be reaped. The field is valuable for the crop that it will yield in spite of the useless refuse that will have to be thrown out later. Harvest time will be the occasion for sorting the valuable produce from the worthless. 'The harvest is the completion of the cycle of time.'

In the following parable it is said of the field that a treasure is hidden, there worth all that a man has. The kingdom of heaven itself is compared to this treasure.

Another parable follows directly after, which speaks in quite a different way of the kingdom of heaven. Here it is represented in the picture of a merchant coming from afar to seek in this world the best of pearls. He finds it here and gives his all to possess it. The true nature of the field is made plain in the contrast. The kingdom of heaven has allowed a portion of itself to remain in this world, but hidden below the surface. It has become a secret treasure, lost unless it is sought and discovered by someone who knows that it is to be found and has the energy to search. Nevertheless the kingdom in its other nature is not of the earth but of the world beyond. It is not in this sense the treasure but the seeker of treasure. The pearl is that which the visiting merchant hopes to find in the place of earth.

The final parable speaks of this world as the sea into which the net is cast. The kingdom of heaven is like the net which brings up fish of every kind. No discrimination is made while the net is out, but when it is drawn into the shore the sorting out of good and bad is done. Nothing is said of how it happens that both good and bad creatures are to be found in the sea of this world. The parable makes the point that, although both are there together as a matter of course, this situation will one day be changed. The time of the harvest will come inevitably in the future. That which has lasting value will be separated from that which will disappear in time, the good from the bad.

This world is the field where man is at work, but it has in fact an owner, an absentee landlord, who is God himself. These parables following one after another, the last three of the seven in the thirteenth chapter of St Matthew's Gospel, form a picture of the relation of this world to the kingdom of heaven. The two are separated but they have to do with one another. Once, at the beginning, heaven and earth were not apart as they are now. When the creating beings of the universe made the earth, its existence was enfolded in theirs, protected within the divine order. The separation came about through the interference of the powers of evil. The earth became so changed that it fell away from the place of its origins into an existence of its own. A void divided it and continues to do so from the life of the heavens. Many things can happen in this world that are excluded from the divinely ordered universe. There the will of God prevails thoroughly and entirely. Here it is restrained. It works only in the life of the stones, the plants and the animals, but human beings are left to deal with their own affairs.

However, into the space left open for the exercise of the human will, the beings of evil have entered intent upon aims of their own. The workers of evil belong to the world of spirit, and are themselves spiritual in their nature. But they have been prevented from pursuing their aims in the heavens and have been thrown back upon the opportunities offered by the earth.

Behind the protection given by the void they can expand their activity in the place from which the direct operation of the will of God has been withdrawn. Where man is at liberty to act, so are they. If their liberty would be curtailed, so would that of man – who would be prevented under such conditions from making his own history. The world of earth has become a place where anything can happen. Because it offers every opportunity to man, the powers of evil have come to take their chance likewise.

The three parables of the treasure, the pearl and the net are a study in the new relationship between the kingdom of God and the world of earth, which has been brought about by the coming of Christ. Before that event, the separation continued to widen – to the dismay and grief of all those in the ancient world wise enough to realise it. Human existence was felt to be in great, increasing danger. The coming of the promised God was expected as mankind's only hope. The Jews awaited the Messiah for many generations. But when the time actually approached they had become confused between the hope of salvation for their race and the pressing need of mankind as a whole. They were in reality not alone in their expectation, although they were the people chosen to prepare the body in which the Messiah would take on human form. Among all the peoples of the ancient world the longing to know that God had come at last was urgently felt. The whole dilemma of mankind roused their strongest concern. But many of the Jews, hindered by narrow national feeling, did not recognise the Messiah when he appeared. He responded to human needs in the highest sense. He came to change the relationship between heaven and earth, between God and man. The pictures in the three parables illustrate what the change was to be.

'The kingdom of heaven is like a treasure hidden in a field.' Although the earth has been separated from the universe, the field shut in by a thick hedge, a heavenly treasure is buried there. From whence did it come? Who hid it? Looking back to the world's beginning, to what took place before the great separation, heaven and earth were one. Heaven gave its substance to the earth. It was God-willed and God-made. A spiritual treasure was laid into its innermost being. Whatever happened later, however far the earth fell away into a devil-ridden existence, the treasure was still there. It was buried out of sight, but it was not destroyed. For its sake the immense labour of world-creation was undertaken and, when completed, given over by the creating gods to the perils of separation. What kind of treasure would be precious enough to make worthwhile such an undertaking? Why should the kingdom of heaven hide a portion of its being just there where it could only be isolated, unprotected and alone? The kingdom is not identified with the field, although they were one at the creation, but with the treasure which it contains. That must and can only be man.

In outer life human beings are dwellers in the field. In their inner life they bear within them the spirit of God. The field is the place of human evolution, but that which evolves in them is the treasure of the spirit entrusted to them by God. If they would see themselves with the eyes of God, human beings would burn with enthusiasm for their destiny on earth, because of what can evolve in and through them. They would know that the spirit of God within them is the meaning and purpose of their whole existence. This is their own, the essence of their individual being, but they discover it only when they find it hidden in the field of earth. It is not to be found in the life before birth or in the world of sleep, but only here where in the midst of temptation they find themselves. But people are slow to discover the treasure, since each single member of humankind has to find it again on their own. And who, sooner than Christ, has valued the treasure and given all that he had to obtain the field, that he might shelter and cherish it, but Christ himself? When human souls lost sight of it and, not knowing their own value, let themselves be seized by the powers of evil, Christ knew that a treasure of God's spirit lived in them and came to find and keep it. He came to man for the sake of the portion of his spirit which God had lost.

41

'The kingdom of heaven is also like a merchant in search of fine pearls.' The picture has changed its angle. The kingdom is like a man going abroad on a business journey. He is a merchant of discrimination, looking not for quantity but for quality. One pearl of unique value is worth all the rest put together. He is interested in pearls above all other jewels. The pearl is not a stone in the ordinary sense. It is formed within a creature of the water, the oyster. Inside its shell the oyster's body is soft and vulnerable. If a grain of sand or something like it comes in contact with it, the oyster protects itself from pain and injury by exuding from its body a milky substance. This covers the offending object, transforming it into a pearl. The injury causes the oyster to make a jewel, to turn the wound into a thing of beauty. The oyster will not produce a pearl, although the required ingredients are present in its body, unless it has something to overcome.

No precious stone can touch the imagination like the pearl. None could replace it in such a parable. Only it could express that which is of such value to the treasure-seeker that he would sell all that he had to buy it. The merchant from afar is Christ himself. He came to the earth on a quest. He was to find that which of all things in this world could be most valuable to the kingdom of God. He was to obtain it that it might become treasure in heaven. What could this be but man in whom God has implanted so much?

Human beings as they are, we ourselves as we are, could not be deemed so precious as to deserve to be sought by such a treasure-seeker. But human beings as they could become, as they have the opportunity to make themselves, can be compared to the pearl sought by the merchant. In the earlier parable, man could be pictured as he was at birth from the divine world. In this later one, man is seen as someone making of himself more than he was at the beginning. He is exposed to the dangers of evil, but he can become something which he would not have been without the misery of independence and temptation. He can call up forces of transformation from within himself. In overcoming his fallen nature, the pains of his destiny on earth, he can create the pearl from within.

How does the merchant come to pay such a price? From whom does he, coming from the world where man was created, have to buy the pearl? The picture covers a wide span of history. The price is not paid all at once, but again and again through the centuries. Christ gives all that he has, all that he is, to humankind in the struggle to fulfil the purpose of earth's evolution. The power to create, with which he came endowed from the universe into this world; that which was unloosed at the resurrection into the stream of evolving human life, is invested in mankind. He gives all that he has for the pearl which is not yet fully formed and in so doing takes part in the process of transformation. From within man's being, he creates; from without he searches out and he purchases. From whom? The powers of evil have been allowed to interfere in this world to the point of taking possession. Man has been unable to resist. He has been enthralled, until the merchant came to buy him back. They are still permitted to operate. But man has been gifted with the spiritual forces with which to produce, under the stress of interference, the pearl. If Christ would not continue to pay the price through the centuries, that itself might be lost and become the booty of the evil ones. They grab, they do not pay. But Christ gives all that he has for the pearl that is in the making.

This world of earth is known in these parables as a field or piece of ground until the last two, when it is said to be like the sea. The corn-growing land is changed for the watery field of the sea that produces pearls and fishy creatures of all kinds. As nothing is said in the parables without meaning, this must also be significant. The last parable, that of the net cast into the water, tells of the future, of the world's end. The hard body of the earth, giving us the firm ground under our feet, will dissolve away. The next stage beyond the physical is that to which the watery element belongs. The all-absorbing sea is the picture for the condition into which the earth will pass as the dissolution

43

proceeds. Evolution will finish. The last harvest will be gathered, the final selection made of good from bad.

For a very long time in the history of Christianity, it has been customary to foresee at the end of the world the Last Judgment. When, before the Reformation, biblical pictures were painted on the walls of churches, such a scene would be represented over the west door, to be faced by the congregation on leaving. Christ would appear as the world-judge; the souls would be seen weighed on scales, the good would proceed up the golden stair to heaven, the bad be thrown down to a ghoulish set of devils below. Such was the violent end expected to human history. Into this picture the problem intruded itself of those who would have died long before this event. Doctrines quite devoid of common sense arose to explain how decaying bodies would be miraculously put together again, coming from the tombs to stand before the judge. Both paintings and doctrines express the confusion of mind that has for centuries muddled the Christian picture of the Last Things.

Judgment is a reality, but it is not reserved only for the final act. At the end of each day a certain process of sorting out takes place in every soul. The actions and experiences are prepared to be taken over into sleep, to be morally digested there. A review of the day's events before sleeping is most effective when it is made backwards from the end to the beginning. This is so because the process of moral digestion in sleep takes the same course. At the end of each lifetime a greater judgment takes place. So long as there is breath in the body, the opportunity for action and change exists. At the gate of death this ceases to be so. The soul will begin to live in the consequences of what was done and said. The harvest of a whole lifetime is reaped in the hour of death. Judgment is not experienced by the soul just once. Again and again there are times of harvest when the seeds that will be planted for the future will be sorted out from the rubbish that proves useless. There are those who, not content with waiting for the harvests that are gathered as a matter of course at sleep and

Floris Books

Name (BLOCK CAPS): _____ ALL

UK and European customers can be added to our postal mailing list:

Address: _____

Postcode: _____ Country: _____ UK & EUROPE ONLY

All customers can be added to our email list:

Email: _____ ALL

☐ Please send me the Floris Books complete catalogue once. UK & EUROPE ONLY (Digital catalogues available online)

I'd like to receive information on (please tick):

*We will **never** pass your details to anyone else.*

☐ AE Philosophy of the Natural World
☐ AF Philosophy of Human Life
☐ AG Astrology & Cosmology
☐ C Mind Body Spirit
    ☐ CA Holistic Health
☐ AA Christian Spirituality
☐ G Biodynamics & Organics
☐ D Art & Literature

☐ IC Karl König Archive
☐ I Steiner-Waldorf Education
    ☐ IA Waldorf Teacher Resources
    ☐ IB Special Needs Education
    ☐ ID Early Childhood Education
☐ J Parenting & Child Health
☐ L Crafts & Activities

Books for children
☐ K Picture Books *(age 3–6)*
    ☐ KA Elsa Beskow Books
    ☐ KB Picture Kelpies *(Scottish)*
☐ M Story Books & Anthologies *(age 6–10)*
☐ NB Kelpies novels *(age 8–12)*
☐ NC KelpiesTeen *(age 11–14)*

Want to hear about new books and get exclusive discounts? Send us your details. OR Sign up at florisbooks.co.uk and get FREE books!

Floris Books

Floris Books
15 Harrison Gardens
Edinburgh EH11 1SH
UK

Special Deals for Floris Subscribers

Sign up at
florisbooks.co.uk
and get a FREE book
every time you order!

in death, deliberately choose occasions to sort out for themselves the affairs of their destiny and to start afresh.

A consideration of these parables should change the established concept of judgment. The picture of legal proceedings before a judge, who can acquit, condemn and sentence, should give way to that of the harvester, who separates corn seed from chaff, or the fisherman, who sorts out the contents of his net, keeping the good and throwing away the bad. Such harvestings are part of the life of each single person and will culminate in the greatest of them in the hour of death. So it is also in history. There are periods when the seeds of the future are sown and times when consequences result that have been prepared long before. It is not difficult to see that such an event as the French Revolution was inevitable in the years when it happened. It was an outburst long due. At the same time new ideas were involved which, although they were drowned in the bloodbath that followed, were the seeds of much that is thought and intended today. Liberty, equality and fraternity are ideals still unfulfilled and necessary to human progress. Once they were seeds. Now they could be pictured as plants, budding perhaps but not yet in flower. The French Revolution itself was the time of harvest, when much that was old and useless was destroyed, leaving what was vital to survive into our century. It makes no difference to the process that at the time the destructive forces got out of hand. It was an hour of judgment in history when, behind the confusion of appearances, the wheat was being separated from the weeds, the good fish from the bad, the past from the future.

The hour of judgment comes again and again in the course of history. Nevertheless, however far ahead, the world-clock will eventually run down and stop. This world will face the hour of death, just as each single person will in due time. As each will encounter the final harvesting of his life, so the world will meet a final harvest. In this sense there is meaning in the old expectation that a great day of reckoning will be the last event in history. There is now still time in earthly affairs for things to be changed. It cannot yet be estimated how many weeds there will be compared with ears of good corn, how many foul creatures in the sea in contrast to the good. The situation can still change. But this cannot go on forever. Evolution must finish, change cease. This in itself brings the final judgment. The harvest will once and for all be gathered, sorted and estimated. The last word will be said on what is good seed that can be taken over into new world-epochs still out of sight, and what is only fit to be destroyed in the great world-death.

The outcome of the harvest can be foreseen before the corn is cut. So the time of decision goes before the hour when the consequences are gathered to a conclusion. The sower has prepared for the reaper. The harvesting is the final act of a long process, the culmination of what went before. It confronts us as a crisis unless we have been aware of how it was prepared in our thoughts and actions. The judgment at the day's end, at life's end and at the world's end is a confrontation from outside with what began inside ourselves. We reap because we have sown. No one comes from outside to condemn or to punish. The situation that we have made faces us that we may judge. There is no mistaking what is to be gathered in and what is to be thrown out. The facts speak for themselves. They can no longer be glossed over. The harvest of a lifetime is the facing of the facts that belong to oneself. The harvest of history is the facing at world level of the facts that belong to all mankind.

Christ is said to be the judge at the world-judgment. It would be more true to say that, as he is the sower of the seed, he will be master of the harvest. He came into this world from across the dividing void. He came to seek mankind and he has remained here to guard and inspire the course of human history. But there were those who rejected him and wished to dismiss him from the earth by killing him. He accepted their judgment and descended into death. In so doing he brought forth the new life of the Resurrection. Instead of leaving the earth, he was born as a spiritual being into the life of mankind through the act of

Resurrection and lives on to guard the course of history until its ending. He cares for the harvesting of what is good and capable of further growth in the worlds of spirit. He separates the weeds from the wheat, the bad fish from the good, that the good may not be lost. When earth-existence dies away, the good seed could die with it. Then its meaning and purpose within the evolution of worlds would be lost. Christ rescues the seed for that which it is intended in the mind of God. He does not condemn, but he puts what is useless aside and gathers that which will outlast the end of the world.

To the way of thinking that inspired the old creed, Christ is expected to appear as the judge who will sentence and condemn in just such a manner as that in which he himself was once tried and condemned in Jerusalem. He is pictured as the great avenger. In our time there is the opportunity to advance to a new picture. Christ intervenes in human history for the sake not of judgment but of resurrection, not to punish the bad but to give lasting life to the good. His presence in human life gives the power to resurrect to that in our thought and action which resembles the good wheat in the field and the good fish in the sea. It draws into the stream of his own Resurrection the souls of those who are united in the effort to transform themselves into the true image of man, which is beheld in him. Those who have a feeling for resurrection, an enthusiasm for becoming, need fear no evil, for he will lead them on the way to their fulfilment. His aim for the world's end is Resurrection.

Christ is the guide of mankind through history, but he does not save human souls from the risks of freedom. At the world-harvest the facts will be faced. There are those who will rise at the death of this world with Christ. But those who have not lived for this purpose will be left behind. They will have passed this judgment on themselves. There is a scene in the Book of Revelation in which the number of redeemed souls is counted. They are reckoned at one hundred and forty-four thousand. In the arithmetic of the Bible, the number twelve has a quality of its own. It represents the community of mankind. One of twelve is not a person in his own right but the representative of one part of mankind, to which eleven others belong. In such terms, 144,000, so many multiples of twelve, would include every individual soul within the human family. In other words, there is a place for everyone among the redeemed. The path to Resurrection is open to all and everyone. But the decision to take it lies with each one for himself. Not even Christ demands or persuades. He who has sown the seed accepts that at the harvest the worthless may be found among the worthy, the bad with the good. So it is necessary for the development of freedom. He has provided a place for every one among those who attain to Resurrection at the end of the world's history. But each one must take it of his own free will.

What awaits that which proves worthless, those who fall behind in the progress of history? What becomes of the weeds and the foul fish? They are thrown into the fire. Such a fire is not of the earth but is within the domain of the angels. In each parable about the end of the world it is said that the angels, when the harvest is gathered in, have charge of the crop and the catch. They do the sorting and dispose of what is valueless. The cosmic fire is at hand and their part is done when the rubbish has been thrown in. Fire consumes but, when the flame flares up, that which is burnt rises to a new level of existence. The furnace of fire presided over by the angels is a place in the universe where processes of purification take place. Transformation by burning is the fate of all that is thrown out of earth evolution at its ending. There is pain in the burning for it follows on failure. But nothing is said of final destruction. The angels do not accept waste. That which is useless in its present form is to be changed and purified by fire.

The angels do the work of Christ. He is present at every hour of judgment up to the last. He guides the soul who is willing to follow into the world of sleep and out again. He is the soul's leader through the gate of death, where everyone, believing or unbelieving, may meet him. He watches over the harvest of a lifetime, that the good seed shall be gathered into the world of spirit. He is the guardian of world-history, gathering the fruits of each crisis of judgment into the store of good seed that will be harvested at the end of earthly time. Who waits for the fruit of mankind's history on earth? Who but God himself, who will receive the harvest into his hands for the sake of what is to come in world-cycles of time. How much does he value it? He who sent his Son to give all that he had for the treasure in the field, for the pearl of great price. What more could he give?

The Good Samaritan

The word 'quest' is one part of 'question' and both are descended from a Latin verb meaning to 'seek'. To go on a quest is to set out on the search for something unknown or at least out of reach. To ask a question is to go in search of an answer to something unexplained or not understood. Both start from the open door, giving on to what is beyond and which must be explored. The ability to ask questions points to an open mind. The tendency to form conclusions means closing the mind on a thought now grasped and settled. In all spiritual matters asking questions has great value but not just 'any questions'. There is skill in asking, handling and finding the answer to them. Nowhere can skill of this kind be better observed than in the gospels, more especially in the conversations of Christ Jesus with those around him.

Luke 10:25–37

> *Then a teacher of the Law stood up to dispute with him and said, 'Teacher, what must I do to win a share in the eternal life?' And he said, 'What is written in the Law, what have you read there?' He answered, 'Love the Lord your God with all your heart and with all your soul and with all your strength and with all your thinking, and love your neighbour as you love yourself.' And he said to him, 'You have given the right answer; act in accordance with it, and you will find life.'*

> *But he wanted to justify himself and said to Jesus, 'And who is my neighbour?'*
>
> *Then Jesus answered, 'Once, a man was going down from Jerusalem to Jericho and he fell into the hands of robbers. They robbed him of his clothes, beat him half dead and left him lying there helpless, and ran off. And it so happened that a priest was going down that same way. When he saw him he walked on past him. So, too, a Levite who was on that road walked past him when he saw him lying there. But then a Samaritan came by. When he saw him he had compassion on him, went up to him, bandaged his wounds, pouring on oil and wine, set him on his own beast, took him to an inn and looked after him. And the next day he took out two denarii, gave them to the innkeeper and said, "Take care of him, and any expenses you have I will refund you when I come back." Which of these three, do you think, proved neighbour to him who had fallen into the hands of the robbers?' He answered, 'The one who showed compassion on him.' And Jesus said to him, 'Go and do likewise.'*

Such a conversation was the circumstance in which the parable of the Good Samaritan was told (Luke 10). A lawyer made his appearance to put a leading question. The evangelist telling the story says he did so in order to put Christ Jesus to the test. He leaves it open whether he acted from bad will or whether he wished to satisfy himself that this new master had principles worthy of respect. Each reader will decide for himself if the scene opened in a mood of bad or good will. The question put was one of the utmost importance: what shall I do to inherit eternal life? Clearly, the idea of eternal life in itself presented a problem to the lawyer. It was not something to be taken for granted, but to be planned for and intended. He did not say, 'Shall I believe in eternal life?' but, 'How can I be sure of having it?' Christ Jesus replied to the question with another of his own, directed straight to the lawyer's special field of knowledge. He asked what was said in the Law. He was well versed in his profession and answered at once with the correct citation. Christ accepted the reply, adding, 'Act in accordance with it, and you will find life.' He gave in fact no answer but the one that the lawyer thoroughly well knew already. He threw him back upon himself.

The conversation did not stop there, because a change of heart had begun to take place in the lawyer. In the beginning he had not taken his own question quite seriously. He had used it as a means to an end. But Christ's way of returning the question back to the questioner had woken him up to its real importance. Moreover, as he asked, he had become more aware of him with whom he spoke. He began to realise his own limitations, perceiving that in reality it was he himself who was being tested. His consciousness was awakened at a higher level of mind and he asked a genuine question, opening himself to a new answer that would transcend what he already knew. Christ recognised the change of heart and this time he replied. He told the story of the Good Samaritan.

There was a certain person. Was he not anyone in particular? Or was he someone so representative that he could stand for anybody, an 'Everyman'? Several kinds of interpretation can come to mind. He left Jerusalem behind him and set out for Jericho. And he went alone. Jerusalem was the centre of the Jewish faith. The Temple was there, in which originally the tablets of stone inscribed with the Commandments had been kept in the Holy of Holies. The priests congregated round the holy place, with the choicest of the scribes and Pharisees, who were the guardians of faith and morals, representing most thoroughly the authority of the Law. To leave Jerusalem was to put oneself outside the protection as well as the order for which they stood. By contrast, shortly before the time when the events in the Gospels took place, Jericho has become the favourite residence of the kings of Herod's line. They were false kings from the strictly Jewish point of view, owing their authority to support from Rome.

Jericho was much favoured by Cleopatra, on whom the right of ownership was once bestowed for a time by the Herod of the moment. It was a place with a great fascination, having a luxuriant climate and vegetation, although being close to the desert at the northern end of the Dead Sea. Its history went right back to Sodom and Gomorrah, ancient cities famous for luxury and wickedness, which were destroyed in a violent natural catastrophe. They were held ever after to have been justly smitten by the wrath of God. There remained, as a last remnant of this very fertile countryside, just Jericho with its much-praised gardens. What could be a greater contrast to Jerusalem than this resort, decadent but fascinating, offering the best of all surroundings for escape from the fanatical faith and stern duty represented by Jerusalem? It stood in the world of that time for everything that could be expected of a place given over to idleness and dissipation. The person who left Jerusalem to go to Jericho was deliberately courting many kinds of danger.

The traveller seems to have gone alone, unusual for someone in those days, especially when he was taking a road known for its dangers. It is possible to imagine various reasons for the behaviour of this person, bent on leaving his workaday world for the pleasures of what could be called the most renowned holiday haunt of the period. Did not Herod long try in vain to beguile Cleopatra into leaving Jericho and returning to Egypt? But one fact stands out beyond discussion. This person took foolhardy risks. He showed neither foresight nor circumspection. He expected to be able to manage by himself but in fact he showed poor judgment.

He fell among thieves, which many people might have said was to be expected. The brigands were out and about. The road gave them good chances against a lonely traveller. They took everything that he possessed and wounded him severely. It is to be supposed that he put up a fight and so was injured. Whether he lived or died does not seem to have concerned the thieves, since they did not stay to finish him off. But he was quite helpless, probably unconscious, since it is not said that he was able to ask for help from those who passed by.

After the attack three people came upon the scene, one after the other, each alone. The parables have a style all their own. They use the language of ordinary life, but they change it into the expression of realities that are not of this world. The customs of the times would have made it unlikely that a series of travellers would come alone. That they are said to have done so is an important part of the story's meaning. Each one was separated from the group upon which he naturally depended. He was on his own in an unexpected situation. From the moment when the certain person set out from Jerusalem to Jericho, the tale is of individual decisions made one after the other. It is a real question what kind of resolve it was from which the events started. It seems to have in it the reflection of the original Fall of man, when human beings began on earth to go their own way, leaving behind them the world-order of God that had been their shelter – and encountering in consequence the powers of evil.

In which direction was the priest travelling, and later the Levi, who were members of the Jewish caste? The reader has to look into the situation for the answer. In all likelihood they were both going towards Jerusalem. They belonged there, within the framework of its order, protected by the customs prescribed by the Law. Their minds were conditioned to it. Once outside the city, they still only knew how to behave according to its regulations. In a strange situation they were helpless, without a proper plan of action. The priest simply took the line of least resistance, passing by on the other side. The Levite saw what had happened, stopped to look, did not apparently know what to do and went on his way. Were they without any feelings of pity? Did they assume that the wounded man had brought it on himself and deserved his fate? Or were they at a loss because they could find no regulation to fit the case? Each reader will interpret the story according to his own way of thinking, for the text does not include explanations. There can be no doubt that the victim on the roadside was in dire need, that the passers-by saw this and did nothing to help.

The third comer was the Samaritan, a citizen of the nation most hated by the Jews of Jerusalem, whose enmity was often returned. Samaria, lying between Judea and Galilee, had a strange history. Its people were not Jewish, having been planted in the land by a conqueror from Babylon. But they had adopted the Law of Moses and the worship of Yahweh because they held the belief of their age that the inhabitants should honour the God of the country. Strict Jews could not endure the claim of these people of foreign origin to share the worship of Yahweh. The Samaritan in the parable is described as a free-minded man, able to stand clear of the usual prejudice. He saw only the need of the ill-used person lying by the road. He responded at once. He disinfected the wounds with wine and treated them with oil to make them heal. He lifted the sufferer onto his beast and took him to the nearest inn. In those days there was no distinction between the place where travellers were entertained and that which catered for the sick and needy. He gave him into the care of the keeper of the hospice and offered to pay the charges.

The traveller was rescued. He would be cared for until he was well and strong enough to set out again. He did not need to be anxious about the cost. It is just as interesting to notice what the Samaritan did *not* do for the man whom he had rescued, as what he is *did* do. The traveller had lost all that he possessed. His plans were at a standstill. He would have to start again from nothing. But the Samaritan did not take him to his own home, offer him a job, propose to replace what he had lost or try to set him up in life again. He did not offer to take charge of him, to be either a friend or patron. He saw to it that he would be restored to the strength with which to help himself and did not interfere in any sense with what he would make of the new situation. He restored him to himself and left him to continue in his own way. If the Samaritan thought that the man had been foolish, or careless, or in any way deserving of his fate, he does not seem to have said so. Here was someone in such need that he could not help himself. He must be put on his feet again, so that he could tackle his own problems.

The Samaritan had compassion. He judged the traveller by the measure of his need. He accepted the need of the other as his affair because their paths had crossed. They had not met before; they might never meet again. But by the roadside they were neighbours – the one helpless, the other able to help. Custom would have justified the Samaritan in passing by a stricken citizen of Jerusalem. But he was not a creature of custom. His heart burned with a compassion not bred by custom and law. 'Help is needed. It must be given. I am here, therefore it is for me to help.' Thus, according to his behaviour, he must have thought. He faced all the consequences of his generous impulse realistically. He made himself responsible for the traveller's stay at the inn, although he could not foresee what sum would be required. No one could know how long it would take the injured man to recover but he guaranteed the cost in advance to the host of the inn. He showed imagination in assessing his own relationship to the one whom he wished to help, knowing just where to stop. What can one person do for another? How far can he live his life for him? When must he step back and say to the other: now you have to do something for yourself. The behaviour of the Samaritan is the pattern of true compassion. It shows the three necessary elements – the good will to recognise the need, the good sense to know what should be done and to do it, and the imagination to realise when to stop.

Compassion is something that lives in the heart. It is awakened when the heart is open to what is going on above and beyond its own inner world. It grows strong where the need is great and wise in perceiving where help is to be given and how. It is made real in action. From whence does it come? What feeds and sustains it? Does everyone discover it when he looks into his own heart? It has a history of its own. It has not always been part of the life in the human soul. When the Buddha appeared in India, five hundred years before the coming of Christ, he preached about compassion to people who had no notion of it. So strange it seemed to the minds of his hearers that he told stories, many of them, one after another, to illustrate it by examples. Most of the tales were about animals of different kinds – monkeys, deer, elephants, swans, dogs and jackals. All told of the same happening: of a great and strong leader of flock, pack or herd, who gave his life for some weaker and smaller one among his followers. Often a human character was involved in the plot, such as a king who had to learn from the animal-hero that wisdom and strength are not the only qualities needed for rulership. As the Buddha told his tales, he was preparing the way for One greater than himself who was still to come.

Older than compassion in human history is law. The relationships between people used to be regulated and often still are by laws laid down and customs enforced within the community. Early laws all had their origin in divine inspiration. The Law of Moses was held in respect because it came directly from Yahweh. Nowadays laws are man-made. But both kinds, old and new, have this in common, that they regulate duties and relationships from outside, demanding certain kinds of behaviour. They are not concerned with the inner place of the heart, with its stirrings of feeling or its forces of imagination, or with the interest of one person in another. It is only of importance that the regulations are carried out.

When the lawyer stood up to question Jesus Christ, on the occasion when the story of the Good Samaritan was told, the first answer that he received pointed to the Law given by Yahweh. When he replied with a saying quoted from it, Jesus Christ accepted the answer as sufficient. It was only when the lawyer himself continued to ask further that he was told of the inner force of compassion, through which the heart could see, feel and act beyond the limits of the Law. Furthermore, he heard, by means of the parable, that the time had already come when the Law, in which he had trusted, would not suffice. It could not give direction on how to deal with the kind of dilemma that would henceforth face mankind. Those who relied on its authority only would become as helpless as the priest and the Levite to do what they would wish to do and what should be done. The time was coming when the heart would have to solve the problems beyond the range of the Law. The stirring of change moved in the lawyer's soul, urging him on to the decisive question from which emerged the parable of the Good Samaritan. Was it a blind urge? Did he realise what he was doing? Was he still out to prove and criticise? Did he know that he was making history, for that, indeed, he was doing.

The parable is a story thought, composed and told by Christ himself. It was at the time more powerful than the tales of the Buddha because it did not only speak about compassion, it was the very fulfilment of the ideal itself. He who told the story was himself the source and origin of that force of the heart of which he was telling. He, God in man on earth, shared a spiritual capacity with the human soul, which had not before descended from the divine to the human.

The Law had been given by Yahweh as a Commandment to be received from above and obeyed. Compassion is a divine attribute entrusted to a person's inner self, with which to fashion his own relationship to the people around him, his neighbours. Under the Law the neighbours would have been the next of kin. Duty towards them was defined and established after the degrees of kinship. By virtue of compassion, there can be no fixed relationships, nor scale of obligations. The neighbour becomes the person nearest at hand. Neighbourliness becomes capable of many forms and changes, according to the need of the one who is nearest, according to respect for the urge to be alone, according to the desire to share and exchange. Who is nearest and dearest is no longer fixed from outside, whether by common custom or by kinship. It is decided freely by those who can take responsibility for themselves. The Samaritan in the story recognised as his neighbour the next person to be in need of his help. Had the traveller not fallen among the thieves, he and the Samaritan might very likely have passed each other by with a mere greeting on the road.

It is Christ himself who has given to us our sense of compassion, for he it was who first acted under its inspiration when he descended from the realms of the Father in heaven to the world of man on earth. Who, in the last resort, is it who fell among the thieves but man himself? Excluded from the divine order of the universe, allowed by the will of God himself to go on his own way of history on earth, he was not able to withstand the interference of the two powers of evil, whose names are Lucifer and Ahriman. They set out to rob him of that which had been made over to him at his creation by the sons of God who gave him of their substance. They turned him into a spoilt poor creature compared with the bright image of his beginning. He was left without even the means of helping himself. How could this be? If God created man, why did he leave him to such a fate? Why did he not prevent and protect? Why so great a risk?

The story of the good Samaritan lets us assume that there were many citizens of Jerusalem who stayed at home and did not fall among the thieves. But they did not meet the Good Samaritan either. Likewise, there are many sons of God who have never left the protection of the order prevailing in the universe. They 'stand before the throne of God and serve him day and night' as it is said in the Book of Revelation (8:15). Something is required of man that their service cannot produce. He may not live entirely and only as he was made at the beginning. He is asked to bring out of himself a new quality, which grows and develops from within. Before it can be created, he must lose that with which he started, which was given to him from outside without his effort.

The turning-point in the story of man, as in the parable, is the fresh start which the traveller will be able to make when he has been healed of his hurts and is ready to stand on his own feet. For God did not give up hope of man when he had fallen so far below himself. He who had created the world in order and wisdom added that which had not been given at the beginning, the virtue of compassion. With compassion, Christ came to deliver man from the thieves. He brought to him, and made him aware of, the inner working of the self. He set him upright. He gave him the means of taking his history into his own hands; he gave him the responsibility for his future, promising to share it with him to the end of the world. He made a new man of the broken-down traveller. Then he turned to man, whom he had raised up, and said, 'Go and do likewise.'

Parables of Faith

Faith is much spoken of in the Gospels. It is neither explained nor defined but it is described. The phrase 'Your faith has made you whole' is found again and again where healings are related. It is spoken of as something active, filling a person's heart and mind from within, expressing itself through the will. It seizes on the thinking, illuminating it with understanding, on the feeling, thrilling it with enthusiasm, and is fulfilled finally in action. The disciples of Christ, from living day by day so near to him, began to see for themselves that they could only follow him out of its strength. They put the request: 'Strengthen our faith.' They must have felt that faith was not something that a person could have and keep, but a growing thing that must be cared for and made to thrive. It should be tended as a gardener does his plants. The request might be put in this way: 'Be the gardener of our soul's garden and make our faith to flourish.'

When speaking of faith, Christ Jesus used pictures that say not so much what it is but how it works. Where they are in the form of parables, they do not begin, as do many others, 'The kingdom of the heavens is like ...' They are in fact not speaking of that theme but of another – of the conditions within the human soul itself. They are in the style of stories that illustrate rather than explain. Furthermore, they are put in relation to events that bring other points to the same theme. The parables illustrate, the events demonstrate, and short passages of teachings are set between. Those who were present at the time must have felt the picture of faith changing continually before their eyes.

Luke 16:1–13

And he said to the disciples, 'A rich man had a steward of whom he heard that he was squandering his property. He sent for him and said to him, "What is this that I hear about you? Give account of your house-management; you shall not remain in your post any longer." Then the steward said to himself: What shall I do if my master takes my job from me? I am not able to do manual work, and I am ashamed to beg. I know what I will do, so that people will take me into their homes when I am removed from my post. And he called all those who were in debt to his master to him, one at a time; and he said to the first, "How much do you owe my master?" He answered, "A hundred kegs of oil." And he said, "Here, take your bill, sit down and quickly write fifty." Then he asked another, "How much do you owe?" He answered, "A hundred measures of wheat." And he said, "Here is your bill, write eighty." And the master pointed out how cleverly the dishonest steward had acted, and he said, "The sons with earthbound minds are cleverer in their way than the sons of the light." I say to you: Use to make friends for yourselves those merely earthly goods which have been hoarded unjustly, so that when they are all used up you will be received into the eternal dwelling-places of the spirit.

Whoever proves trustworthy in small things is also trustworthy in great things; and whoever does wrong in small things also does wrong in great things. And if you do not prove trustworthy in your dealings with merely earthly goods, unjustly hoarded, will you then be entrusted with the true riches? If you do not prove trustworthy with things which are essentially foreign to you, will anyone then give you that which concerns us here? No servant can serve two masters simultaneously; either he will hate the one and love the other, or he will be attached to the one and despise the other. You cannot serve both God and the powers of all merely earthly existence at the same time.'

They must have seen the true living idea first from one angle and then another and found it always just out of reach. But at some moment the realization would dawn that faith is something that lives within one's own heart. The sick who were healed with the help of their faith must have prepared it long before within themselves. Perhaps they never recognised until it was called forth at the time of their healing how much had already grown and ripened.

Faith begins with the realization that the soul has inner powers that can emerge into activity. The first parable in this series tells of a steward who was accused of dishonesty in his office. He seems to have been quite aware of his guilt and to have wasted no time on self-defence. He accepted that all was up with him as a steward and faced the disaster with just one question: what shall I do? This parable is a puzzle in that it seems to speak with approbation of a thoroughly dishonest person. Having cheated in his job, he proceeded to cheat on a still grander scale. Using the last hours of his authority with effect, he reduced the debts of all those who owed something to his master. He thereby transferred part of their obligation to himself. The debtors would be obliged to take him as a guest into their houses when he finally lost his job. 'I am not able to do manual work, and I am ashamed to beg,' he decided, when he deliberated on the matter. One would expect the owner to be annoyed at being so cheated, but on the contrary he appreciated the steward's cleverness and still more his prompt action in looking out for himself. The owner was left, cheated indeed, but able to dismiss the steward without being responsible for making him a beggar.

If we assume that in this story the owner represents the kingdom of heaven, as is the custom throughout the parables, then does the conclusion follow that God accepts dishonesty? The owner is said to have commended the steward for refusing to lapse into beggary and for having solved the situation for himself. His dishonesty is not praised but his self-reliance. He used his intelligence to oblige other people to make a place for him in their lives. He refused to be dropped or overlooked. Losing one destiny he made another. But he cheated. The parable is followed by a passage that is in a sense part of it, in so far as it brings the antidote to the spectacle of successful dishonesty. It speaks of the contrast between God and mammon (or the 'powers of merely earthly existence' in the quoted translation).

Mammon is a mysterious expression in the Gospels. Just here in the parable it carries the adjective 'unrighteous' or 'unjust'. God is the being of righteousness, Mammon of unrighteousness. It is a matter of fact that either one is served or the other. In order to translate this general idea into practical experience one may turn to the portrait of an archangel. In Rudolf Steiner's world-picture, archangels are beings of God who weave their influences into the fabric of human life in continuous activity. They are to be distinguished from one another by differences of character and task. The archangel Uriel is noted for his gaze, for the clear look that he casts into human affairs, beneath which what is righteous is separated from what is unrighteous. He is by nature the guardian of righteousness, before whom no shadow of unrighteousness can be hidden or excused. We feel the reflection of his gaze in our human hearts when we are satisfied with a just action or indignant at a piece of injustice. We, with our limited minds, feel the distinction, but Uriel penetrates with his gaze to the facts that underlie our moral feeling. He looks into the spiritual life of the earth, into the depths where the harmonious interplay of forces in the stones and minerals form its foundation.

The substance of rocks and stones does not endure. It is continually being eaten away. But the mathematical forces that shape them are enduring. They reflect the harmonious order of the universe itself in the depths of the earth. We feel ourselves upheld and sustained by it. Furthermore our inner sense of justice finds here its foundation. The harmonious architecture of the earth has a moral counterpart when righteousness prevails in human affairs. Unrighteous actions, impulses of self-seeking, damage the edifice of human relationships. They hinder the temple of God from being built on earth, while righteous thoughts and actions are raising it up. You cannot serve God and mammon, because you are engaged in either destroying or building the temple. Each action is doing one or the other but, clearly, not both at once.

The archangel Uriel with his powerful gaze looks upon the right architecture of forms in the earth's foundation of rocks and minerals, and compares with them the forms produced by human behaviour. Our sense of justice may weaken in the struggles of existence, our feeling for right behaviour may tire, but the gaze of Uriel has its effects in the depths of our soul-life. He does us the great service of renewing our sense of right, which we have direct from our connection with the divine world, the substance of whose being is righteousness. If we lose our feeling for what is right, we would be cut off in our whole nature from the divine. Uriel serves the good of mankind with his own particular virtue. The devotion of his whole will as an archangel is poured into the gaze with which he looks towards God, absorbing into himself the revelation of righteousness in the universe. The same intense gaze is turned in due time towards man's life on earth. There he beholds in the depths, in the forms of stones and crystals, the harmony of the heavens. Between the heights and the depths human existence on earth is outspread. It can be imagined with what a contrast it must appear to the gaze of Uriel. Above and below the harmony of rightness throws into relief the confusion of right and wrong in between. Human history is composed of the struggle between right order and chaotic distortion. Uriel looks down and right is sifted from wrong, good is accepted and bad is rejected in his gestures. Beneath his gaze moral discrimination, the taste for righteousness is renewed in human hearts.

What might seem abstract in the expression 'righteousness' ceases to be so when one imagines how the world is seen under the gaze of Uriel, who devotes himself to calling the people on earth to the service of God. Mammon – the powers of all merely earthly – is the state of the world in which unrighteousness prevails instead of harmony, where distorted forms are produced by the impulse of self-seeking. Every piece of unrighteousness, when its deepest cause is found, depends on the urge to promote one's own ends to the exclusion of everything else. Just as Uriel endeavours to inspire our vision of rightness, so other spiritual beings foster our unrighteous longings. Lucifer and Ahriman, the Princes of Evil, are at hand to prompt us to make the temple of mammon here, where the temple of God should be built. When their promptings are followed, mammon thrives a little more. When the gaze of Uriel is followed, the love of righteousness increases. God and mammon cannot be anything but opposites.

Luke 16:19–31

'Once there was a rich man, dressed in purple and fine
linen. Every day he held splendid and merry feasts. And
a poor man named Lazarus lay in front of his entrance
hall, covered with sores, and begged for the scraps from the
rich man's table to still his hunger. And the dogs came and
licked his sores. Now the poor man died and was carried
by angels to Abraham's bosom. And the rich man also died
and was buried. And in the realm of shadows, where he
had to endure great suffering, he lifted up his eyes and saw
Abraham from afar, and he saw Lazarus in his bosom.
And he called out: "Father Abraham, have mercy on me
and send Lazarus to dip his fingertip in water and cool
my tongue with it, for I am suffering in this flame!" But
Abraham said, "My son, remember that you had goods
in your earthly life; but Lazarus only had what was bad.
Now he is receiving comfort for his soul here, and you are
suffering. And what is more, a great chasm separates us
from you; no one wanting to cross from here to you is able
to do so, nor can anyone pass from there to us." Then he

*said, "Then I beg you, father, to send him to the house
of my father, for I have five brothers. I want him to be
a witness to the truth for them, so that they do not also
come to this place of torment." But Abraham said, "They
have Moses and the prophets; let them hear them." He
replied, "No, father Abraham, if someone rises from the
dead and comes to them, then they will change their hearts
and minds." But he said, "If they do not heed Moses and
the prophets, neither will they heed one who rises from the
dead".'*

The parable of the unjust steward seems to praise someone
who successfully serves mammon. But another parable follows
immediately. The story of Dives and Lazarus stands by itself,
but one of its features is important here in relation to what goes
before. The rich man and the beggar are said to have lived side by
side in this world. Dives enjoyed all that belonged to the realm
of mammon. He did not behave badly by his own standards
of decency. He shared the pleasures of riches with his relatives
and fed the beggar at the gate. In the life after death the just
consequences of his way of life and that of the beggar followed.
He was tormented with selfish longings that could no longer
be satisfied and Lazarus entered the spheres of peace, where
righteousness makes harmony in the soul-world. It is said that the
rich man appealed to the guardian-spirit of his people, Abraham,
who was sheltering Lazarus, to relieve his suffering. But the just
order of existence could not be changed even by Abraham. There
can be no misunderstanding about the first parable, when it is seen
beside the second. 'And yet it is more possible for heaven and earth
to pass away than for even one dot of the Law to become invalid.'
These words of Jesus Christ are the link between these parables, of
which one supplements the other.

The choice between God and mammon is found in this
world, but not in the life after death, in the world of God. The
passage of teaching between the two parables discusses the great

riddle of existence, that man is given a space during his life on earth in which he need not live in righteousness. The just consequences are bound to come in time but meanwhile he takes his choice and sets his own standards. How does it come about that he is put into so dangerous a situation, where he can do so much damage? The unrighteous mammon has a function in human history without which man could not develop the full power of his humanity.

In St Luke's Gospel (Chapter 15) the story of the Prodigal Son is told in which the whole fate of man has been represented in one picture. One feature should be recalled here. Two brothers are described, an elder and a younger one. The elder is said to have led a protected existence, sheltered in the world where the righteousness of the father prevails. The younger was not intended to be protected. He was sent out to become independent in the far-off world where he would face temptation, where he could fall into error, but where he would nevertheless find himself. To become independent is part of man's true humanity. He cannot do so when he is sheltered in the divine righteousness. But he can do so, when he is placed between righteousness and unrighteousness – between God and mammon. The acquaintance with mammon is necessary to liberate man from God, but it is neither necessary nor intended that man should serve mammon. He should make use of him, taking the opportunity to develop the powers within himself that are produced by the conditions prevailing where mammon rules. The unjust steward is said to have done just that. Had he done his job decently and honourably he would not have learnt how to fend for himself. The Law is nevertheless not made void.

The true attitude to mammon – to merely earthly goods – is described in the words of Christ that follow the story of the unjust steward. 'If you do not prove trustworthy in your dealings with merely earthly goods, unjustly hoarded, will you then be entrusted with the true riches?' In the realm of mammon the qualities can be developed that will only grow in conditions of self-reliance. With these qualities man will serve God but he will acquire them through mammon.

In a sense our ordinary life today brings us into such conditions. Many a job or profession gives to those who are engaged in it the chance to unfold skill and intelligence and to take responsibilities that foster maturity of character. Very few people can feel that the content of their work has lasting value. Many are wearied by the lack of purpose in what they have to do. But when the qualities that are cultivated through doing such work are considered another significance appears. The journeys of a car-driver may be meaningful or senseless in themselves. Nevertheless the act of driving, of controlling the vehicle, choosing the route and observing the behaviour of other cars, develops abilities that otherwise lie dormant. The journeys may be taken in the service of mammon, but God can be served with the enhanced abilities. 'If you do not prove trustworthy with things which are essentially foreign to you, will anyone give you that which concerns us here?' A person's abilities are in the first place those that we bring, we know not how, with us into this world when we are born. What we make of them by our energetic use is our own. From the point of view of God, each of us doing our best is being faithful with what is another's, that is to say with what has been given to us. But, through our faithfulness, we qualify for what is our own, for becoming someone exercising our will in our own right.

Luke 17:5–19

And the apostles said to the Lord, 'Strengthen our faith!'
And the Lord said, 'If you had faith as a mustard seed, you
could say to this sycamine tree: Be uprooted and be planted
in the sea! And it would obey you.

'Who of you who has a servant for ploughing or for
herding sheep will say to him when he comes home from
the field, "Come at once and sit down at table?" Rather, he

will say, "Prepare the meal for me, put on your apron and wait on me while I eat and drink; afterwards you can eat and drink, too." Does the servant deserve thanks for doing his duty? Think of yourselves like that; when you have done all that you have been told to do, then say: We are feeble servants, we have only done what we were obliged to do.'

And he went on, on his way to Jerusalem, right through Samaria and Galilee. And once, as he came to a village, he was met by ten lepers. They stood at a distance and called with raised voices: Jesus, Master, have mercy on us!' When he saw them he said to them, 'Go and show yourselves to the priests.' And as they went they were healed. But one of them turned back when he became aware that he had been healed, praised the revelation of God with a loud voice, fell on his face at Jesus' feet and thanked him. And he was a Samaritan. Jesus said, 'Were not ten healed? Where are the other nine? Are they not returning to praise the power of God? Why is it only this foreigner who does that?' And he said to him, 'Stand up and go your way; your faith has helped you.'

When the self-reliant activity of a human soul offers itself to the service of God, it becomes faith. Passing from Chapter 16 to Chapter 17, the theme progresses from that of self-reliance to pictures describing faith. The apostles asked Christ to increase their faith. He replied: 'If you had faith as a mustard seed, you would say to this sycamine tree: Be uprooted and be planted in the sea! And it would obey you.' Is faith stronger than the forces of nature? Is that which grows up as independent spirit within the human soul more than that power of divine origin which fashions the tree? When we read in the Book of Job that God answered Job out of the whirlwind, we hear him proclaiming his power and wisdom manifested in nature. When we listen to the answer of Christ to the apostles, we hear him speaking of human faith as greater and more powerful still. Could this in reality be so?

A small parable follows the picture of the tree removed. It describes the servant who, having worked in the fields, serves his master's supper as a matter of course before taking his own. So, we are told, however hard we strive in spiritual matters, we shall be left feeling that we are like servants who have scarcely done our job properly. The two pictures, coming one after another, tell their own story. The tree removed is an ideal belonging to the future, something to aim at as the true maturity of faith that must be one day. Compared with such an ideal, what we achieve now is, at its best, the work of unprofitable servants.

An event is described immediately after these parables in which the theme of faith is illustrated from real life. Between Samaria and Galilee, Jesus Christ met ten lepers, cast out from their village because of their disease. They asked for his help. Perhaps they asked out of habit, as they would have cried out to any one of the wandering healers frequently met with at that time. Perhaps it was quite beyond their expectation to find themselves completely healed. They hurried away to obtain the confirmation from their priests, which would be their passport back to ordinary life. Perhaps they wanted to be reassured by those in authority. One of them came to his senses first, a Samaritan, who turned back while the others hurried off. He returned to give thanks, to acknowledge the divine power which had healed him. What happened to him that was missed by the others? He heard Christ say, 'Your faith has helped you.' The inner strength of the man's faith had been such that the power of Christ could unite with it in the act of healing. The forces of the constitution had been influenced by the warm glow of faith, that the process of degeneration could be transformed into one of regeneration.

In this instance faith has worked just within the sick man's own constitution. Further developed, it would become capable of working into the processes in the world around – for instance, into the behaviour of a tree. On the face of it, the regeneration of a man's dying body might seem to be of greater value than mastery over trees. But the picture has a greater depth. A tree is part of the living body of the earth. The forces of decay are active there as they are in the human body. The creating power of human faith should grow and increase until it can stream beyond the confines of one's own body into that of the earth itself. Man owes his existence in the body to Mother Earth. He should become able to give or return the healing power of human faith that unites with the working of Christ to transform the world.

Luke 17:20–37

At that time the Pharisees asked him, 'When will the Kingdom of God come?' And he answered, 'The Kingdom of God does not come in a form which is outwardly perceptible. Nor does it come in such a way that one can say: Look, here it is, or there. Behold, the Kingdom of God is within you.' And he said to the disciples, 'There will come times when you will long to experience even one of the days of the Son of Man, and you will not experience it. Then they will say to you: Look, there! or Look, here! Do not follow this call, do not go on this path. For the Son of Man in his day will be like the lightning which flashes up in one part of the sky and yet instantly pours out its bright light over the whole firmament. But first he must suffer much agony and be rejected by this present humanity. As it was in the days of Noah, so will it be in the days when the Son of Man will reveal himself: They ate and drank, they came together in marriage as man and wife, until the day when Noah entered the ark and the great flood broke over them and destroyed everything. It was the same in the days of Lot: They ate, drank, bought, sold, planted, built, until Lot left Sodom, and fire and sulphur rained from heaven and everything perished. It will be like that, too, in the days when the Son of Man will reveal himself.
'When that time comes, let him who is on the roof of

> *his house, having left his goods in the house, not go down*
> *to fetch them. And let him who is out in the open field not*
> *go back to what he has left behind. Remember Lot's wife!*
> *For whoever tries to preserve his soul unchanged will lose it,*
> *and whoever is prepared to lose it, will in truth find himself*
> *in the life of the spirit. I tell you: Then there will be two*
> *sleeping at night in one bed; one is gripped by it, the other is*
> *left empty-handed. Two women will be grinding at one mill:*
> *One is deeply stirred, the other is left empty-handed.' And*
> *they said to him, 'Where shall we turn our gaze, Lord?' And*
> *he answered, 'Become aware of your life-body, and you will*
> *see the eagles which are gathering.'*

The juxtaposition of pictures and events in the Gospels speaks in a language of its own. A reader who follows this clue through only a few chapters will find that he begins to see a set of signposts showing paths of thought that could be missed if they went unobserved. Chapter 17 of St Luke's Gospel is a prominent example. Its theme is the request to Christ, 'Strengthen our faith'. What follows, disjointed as it may appear at first, is an answer in a threefold form. Faith, twofold in kind, has been considered. The third revelation of faith is found in the last verses of the chapter, which contain prophetic visions of things to come. Three great crises in history are set forth one after the other, the Flood from which Noah was rescued in the ark, the destruction by fire of Sodom and Gomorrah, from which Lot was saved by walking out in time, and a third great destruction yet to come. The Son of Man will be revealed.

In the great rebirth of the world, which will then take place, what comes from the past and has no value for the future will be discarded. Those human souls who cling to what is valueless will be involved in the destruction. Those who are willing to be reborn with the new time of history will be carried forward to the future. The clue to the significance of the prophecy lies in the words: 'Remember Lot's wife. For whoever tries to preserve his soul unchanged will lose it, and whoever is prepared to lose it, will in truth find himself in the life of the spirit.' Lot's wife is the one who could not leave the past behind, turning back when she should have gone on. Progress is the way through losing to finding, through dying to rising again. Only he who is willing to go this way will follow Christ. His faith will give him the strength to go forward. He will look ahead, 'by the hope of resurrection'. In the light of his faith he will never lose sight of Christ, who leads the way through every experience of losing and finding. Faith that made the lepers whole, that could remove the tree, will bring mankind at last to the resurrection at the end of the world.

With this picture of the time to come the climax is reached in the study of faith but not its conclusion. From the widest perspective of world-history the theme is brought back again to the inner place of the human heart. From the responsibility for world history, Christ leads the thoughts of his hearers back to the responsibility of each one for himself. The next lesson in how to cultivate and use faith begins with the parable of the widow, who went to the judge to ask for judgment against her oppressor. The judge was a powerful man devoid of devotion to justice, but he gave her the assistance to which she had a right – simply because she bothered him continually. 'I will see that this widow gets justice because she will not leave me in peace.'

The first ingredient of faith is persistence. Never to lose heart but to go on without fail is the first instruction of Christ. The second is found in the parable that follows. Two men prayed side by side in the Temple. The one was a Pharisee, so convinced of his own righteousness that he thanked God he was not as other men are. The other was a tax collector who prayed for mercy because he thought of himself as a sinner. The pride of the one is rebuked in the parable; the humility of the other is praised. The second ingredient of faith is the strength of mind to ask oneself how one may look in the eyes of God. Someone may be full of merit in his own estimation or in that of his neighbours and by

divine standards still be in need of mercy. He will find access to
the kingdom of God not by merit but by the energy of his faith.

Luke 18:15–27

*And the people brought their tiny children to him so that he
might lay his hands on them. When the disciples saw this,
they wanted to stop them. But Jesus called them to him and
said, 'Let the children come to me and do not hinder them.
They have the Kingdom of God in their very being. Yes, I
tell you: Whoever does not take the Kingdom of God into
himself as a child has it within him, he will never find the
way into it.'*

*Once, one of the leaders of the people asked him, 'Good
Master, what must I do to attain to eternal life?' And
Jesus said to him, 'Why do you call me good? No one is
good, except the divine Father only. Do you know the
commandments: You shall not corrupt marriage, you shall
not kill, you shall not steal, you shall not bear false witness,
honour your father and mother?' He said, 'All that I have
kept from my youth.' When Jesus heard this answer, he
said, 'Then there is one thing more for you to do. Sell all
your goods and give the proceeds to the poor; thereby you
will acquire a treasure in the spiritual worlds; and then come
and follow me!' These words made him very sad, for he was
extremely rich.*

*Jesus saw it and said, 'How hard it is for those who
have earthly riches to find entry into the Kingdom of God!
It is easier for a camel to go through the eye of a needle than
for a rich man to enter into the Kingdom of God.' Those
who heard this asked, 'Then who can find salvation?' And
he answered, 'What is impossible for human strength will
become possible through the power of God.'*

*Then Peter said to him, 'See, we have left all that was
ours behind us and have followed you.' And he said to them,*

'Yes, I say to you, everyone who leaves a house or a wife or brothers or parents or children for the sake of the Kingdom of God will receive much more in this earthly existence, and, in the coming aeon, deathless life.'

And he took the twelve aside and said to them, 'See, we are going up to Jerusalem, and everything written in the books of the prophets will be done to the Son of Man and so be fulfilled. He will be betrayed to the peoples of the world; be mocked, maltreated, spat on; and when they have scourged him, they will kill him. But then he will rise again on the third day.' But they understood nothing. His words were hidden from them, they did not grasp their meaning.

As he approached Jericho, a blind man was sitting by the wayside, begging. And hearing a crowd going by, he asked what this meant. They told him, 'Jesus of Nazareth is passing by.' And he called out: 'Jesus, Son of David, have compassion on me.' And those who were in front scolded him, telling him to be quiet; but he cried out all the more: 'Son of David, have compassion on me.'

And Jesus stopped and let him be brought to him. And when he came near, he asked him, 'What do you want me to do for you?' He said, 'Lord, let me receive my sight again.' And Jesus said to him, 'Receive your sight; your faith has healed you.'

And immediately he saw again, and he followed him, praising the revelation of God. And all the people saw it and gave praise to God.

Halfway through Chapter 18 the instruction in faith ceases to be given in pictures but continues through happenings. A crowd of little children were brought to Christ. His disciples found it unnecessary. But he pointed out to them how valuable are the forces of childhood. He was not simply admiring the innocence of the children. He was indicating what the child in man, the original child hidden within each grown-up person, means for the life of the spirit. As children accept their life on earth with hope and trust, so the soul opens to the life of the kingdom of God through faith. As the child turns in interest and devotion to what is around him, so the soul should turn to God. In the inner life of the grown person the forces of the child that he has once been, blossom again more consciously and more inwardly. They give him the open mind to see afresh in wonder.

No sooner had the disciples begun to understand the children than, by way of contrast, they met the wealthy ruler, a man of position and of learning in the Law. The children had asked for nothing but to look at Christ and to wonder. The ruler asked outright for the biggest thing of all, eternal life. Christ replied by speaking of the well-known commandments of the Law. The ruler could say that he had always kept them, but showed by his question that he did not expect this to be enough. The next step, he was told, was not to seek for more, but to give up what he already had. 'Sell all that you have and distribute to the poor.' All that he had acquired within and without – knowledge, the authority of position, the skill of experience and his riches – were to be offered to the service of those with less or nothing, the poor. The man was sorrowful. He had much to give him influence in this world and as far as he could see prosperity in the world beyond death. He should give up all this for whom? He should bestow it on those with less or nothing, who would never rise beyond the ordinary.

To give instead of gaining more, to lose instead of finding, to step down instead of up had never been taught in the Law. It was the new teaching of Christ, of which he himself gave the greatest example. From the meeting with the children, the disciples learnt that wonder is the manifestation of faith, when it shines in the thinking. From the encounter with the ruler, they had to realise that to sacrifice one's self is the work of faith in the will. The clear mind and the selfless will are the fruits of faith.

The final scene of the chapter represents the testing of the faith of the disciples themselves. Christ began to tell them of the passion and death that lay ahead of him. They were to understand that the sacrifice asked of the ruler was to be fulfilled by himself in the offering of his life for 'the poor', for the human souls who had lost their divine inheritance. The theme of Christ's life on earth is the offering of the Highest to those who had fallen the lowest, of suffering and death undergone for the sake even of those who inflicted it in blind hate. The disciples could not understand. They could feel for the sadness of the ruler faced with the command to part with his wealth. They could only feel dismay at the thought of parting with their Master in a death of self-sacrifice. What would the poor make out of the riches of one ruler? What would poor humanity gain from the sacrifice of the Son of God himself?

The blind beggar by the wayside gave them their answer. Helpless and useless, an object of charity to passers-by, he had nevertheless insight in his heart and the quality of persistence in the will. He recognised by his footsteps who it was who came by. He called three times above the noise of the crowd. He knew how to ask for the sight which he lacked. The disciples had outer sight, but he had the insight of faith. To him the words were said, 'your faith has healed you.' Faith gives sight, sight gives courage, so the lessons on faith in these chapters conclude. The open mind, the courageous heart, the will to give all, these were shown to the disciples that they should see, hear and grow in understanding. Faith is not something to have and hold. It is a living thing, to be planted as a seed, to grow in patience and to bear in its due time the fruit that ripens in experience.

Dives and Lazarus

It would have to be said of death today that it is the great Unknown. An airman, whose last words were recorded as his plane hurtled down, was heard to say to his crew 'Boys, this is It.' Death is the great 'It' up against which we shall all come, realizing in the event of what quality we are made. That in us which is entirely of this world will come to an end. That which survives will be transformed. The greatest of all tests is indicated by the mysterious word 'It' when it is used in this sense. The ancient Egyptians were more knowledgeable than people of our time commonly are. They had no need to speak of death as 'It'. They had maps and guide books, by which they knew in advance what to expect. Much of their information is to be found in the work known as the Egyptian Book of the Dead. Great stress is laid there on the knowledge of right speaking. Help could be expected from the great gods, whom the human soul would meet on the journey beyond the gate of death, if he knew how to address them with the correct names, what words to say and how to give his voice the right pitch. Without exact knowledge, he would expect to be in poor shape.

After death would come judgment, so it was thought at that time. The human heart would be weighed against a feather. The god who presided on that occasion would be Osiris, he who had once been the sun-god on earth but had himself been slain, becoming then the lord among the dead. He was to be encountered in a temple, where the roof was of fire and the floor of running water. Two goddesses, Isis and Nephthys, held there the Maati or measuring sticks of rightness. A council of 42 gods sat with them and the soul should know the names of each one. They were the recipients of his confession, which was demanded of him so that he might survive the judgment. He had to confess that wrong had not been done in 42 ways, one for each god. These wrongs were of a social nature such as taking what belonged to a neighbour or neglecting duties due to the gods or to the relatives. The soul that could justly make the negative confession in 42 parts was one who had kept the original relationship to the divine world unspoilt. When the soul had then survived the weighing on the scales, it entered the world of the dead, or Amenta, and lived on through its many experiences, which could call to mind the 'many mansions' of heaven spoken of in the Gospels. There he came under the rule of the great god Osiris.

When the Jews of the ancient world thought of death, they likewise had exact notions. They expected, after leaving this life, to encounter not 42 lesser gods under the leadership of a great one but 42 ancestors presided over by the great father Abraham. Yahweh, the god of Israel, had promised to the founder of the tribe that his descendants should be like the stars in the heavens. Was this a picturesque way of saying that they would be very numerous? Rudolf Steiner (lectures on the Gospel of St Matthew) thought that it was more. It meant that the families and the great leaders would carry the virtues of certain constellations among the stars down into their human destinies on earth. They would not live for themselves alone but for the sake of serving the inspirations of the greater sons of God, who live and move among the stars. The twelve tribes of Israel reflected the nature of the twelve signs of the zodiac, that belt of constellations encircling the sky along which the sun travels in the course of the year. Whereas a single person even today can be influenced by the character of the sign under which he was born, each descendant of Abraham entered a tribe bearing the impress of one of the twelve, to which he must remain faithful for life.

The leaders in the history of the Jews were under the influences of the planets, each showing the character of the genius inspiring one or other of the seven. The orchestra of the spheres repeated its music on earth in the deeds, the sayings and the history about which we read in the Old Testament.

The Jewish person of old times expected when his soul left the body in death to enter the world of the stars to meet there the figures among his ancestors who had revealed their inspirations on earth. They were thought to have left a living impress of themselves in that sphere and so to confront the souls of their descendants. The meeting would be a judgment, not unlike that described in the Book of the Dead. The earthly deeds of the soul who had come through death would be measured against the pattern of true human behaviour as it lived in the mind of God. The spirits of his ancestors would measure his character and record against the standards of the divine world. What became of him at the next stage of existence would depend on how he passed the judgment. Again, as in the belief of the Egyptians, it was decisive to be able to say 'I have not done so and so' or 'I have not offended against Yahweh or the people round me.' The Law of Moses reflects the style of this negative confession in the commandments which begin 'Thou shalt not'.

The Gospel of St Matthew opens with a table of the ancestors of Jesus from Abraham downwards. The Gospel of St Luke records another table beginning from Jesus and going back to Abraham, Adam and to God himself. Both are significant in terms of history but even more so as a reflection of what a Jewish soul could experience. The ancestors were the onlookers at the history which was made by each generation and the judges who would pronounce the judgment of God. The rite of baptism which was performed by John the Baptist to prepare the souls of people in his time for the meeting with the Messiah was more than a token of purification. It was a procedure that actually caused a partial separation of the soul from the body, a form of rehearsal for dying. The baptised person had a glimpse of the judgment of the ancestors. But he could, as the dead could not, take up his life on earth again under its awful impression. The list of ancestors is found in the two Gospels in connection with the appearance of Christ on earth. The heavens were opened and the will of God began to be done on earth. The divine standard of judgment began to prevail here as among the ancestors in the heavens.

Is this really so? Even this story is in reality about the way in which two men had behaved on earth, but it goes on further to show how their behaviour looked when seen in heaven. It tells how father Abraham and the ancestors viewed the deeds of the two men by the standard of the just and righteous order prevailing in the spheres of the stars. It does not tell the entire history of the life after death. Reading in the Egyptian Book of the Dead, one finds, after the account of what happened in the Hall of Judgment, a description of the soul's rising up into the new life of Amenta. There the soul was to become a citizen of the universe and dwell with the heavenly hosts who live and move among the stars.

Luke 16:19–31

'Once there was a rich man, dressed in purple and fine
linen. Every day he held splendid and merry feasts. And
a poor man named Lazarus lay in front of his entrance
hall, covered with sores, and begged for the scraps from the
rich man's table to still his hunger. And the dogs came and
licked his sores. Now the poor man died and was carried
by angels to Abraham's bosom. And the rich man also died
and was buried. And in the realm of shadows, where he
had to endure great suffering, he lifted up his eyes and saw
Abraham from afar, and he saw Lazarus in his bosom. And
he called out: "Father Abraham, have mercy on me and send
Lazarus to dip his fingertip in water and cool my tongue
with it, for I am suffering in this flame!" But Abraham said,

> *"My son, remember that you had goods in your earthly life;*
> *but Lazarus only had what was bad. Now he is receiving*
> *comfort for his soul here, and you are suffering. And what is*
> *more, a great chasm separates us from you; no one wanting*
> *to cross from here to you is able to do so, nor can anyone pass*
> *from there to us." Then he said, "Then I beg you, father, to*
> *send him to the house of my father, for I have five brothers.*
> *I want him to be a witness to the truth for them, so that they*
> *do not also come to this place of torment." But Abraham*
> *said, "They have Moses and the prophets; let them hear*
> *them." He replied, "No, father Abraham, if someone rises*
> *from the dead and comes to them, then they will change their*
> *hearts and minds." But he said, "If they do not heed Moses*
> *and the prophets, neither will they heed one who rises from*
> *the dead".'*

According to the old Jewish way of thinking, the dead soul who survived the judgment with success was received into the community by those who lived on under the care of father Abraham. This state of existence after death is called in the language of St Luke's Gospel being in 'Abraham's bosom'. It is said in the parable of Dives and Lazarus that after death the two men who had known each other on earth found themselves in quite separate places of experience. The poor man, who had been a sick and helpless beggar, was taken into Abraham's bosom. The rich man, who had fared well in his life on earth, found himself in a place of torment. The parables are all stories composed and told by Jesus Christ himself. They convey what, from his divine point of view, he wished the human hearts to know and understand. It is significant that the themes of the stories are mostly connected with the meaning of human life on earth, with man's aim and purpose. The parable of Dives and Lazarus, which is told only once in the Gospels, is remarkable for extending the picture of human life from the earth into the world beyond the gate of death. It could be said, put bluntly, that Christ did not come to tell men and women about heaven but about what they should be doing and becoming here on earth. But on one occasion he went further and opened a window in this parable onto the heavens.

There is no parable in the Gospels about human life in the universe. The story of the rich man and the beggar takes their history through the judgment and its aftermath. Lazarus is to be seen in the care of the spirit of Abraham but that is not his ultimate destination. Abraham will pass on his soul in due course to the realms of the Father-God himself and he will begin his journey through the spiritual worlds of the universe. The window opened onto the heavens in this story lets us see the place of judgment and then closes again. The parable tells of two men leading opposite kinds of lives. The one lives in good circumstances surrounded by a crowd of congenial relations. He speaks later of five brothers living in the same opulent style as himself. Their portrait is drawn in sparse but telling words. They wear fine, rich clothes and eat as if they were at a feast every day. The other is poorest of the poor, a beggar covered in sores.

In the custom of old times begging was the proper occupation of those who could not help themselves, and almsgiving the duty of those who had means. It did not carry the stigma of humiliation as it does today. But by begging a person declared himself helpless and dependent, which could be hard to bear, while by almsgiving someone could often improve his public image. The beggar in the parable is accepted at the rich man's gate. He expects the crumbs from the table and he receives them. It is not said that Dives failed in the duty of almsgiving, that Lazarus did not have his share. He does not seem to die of starvation, but neither is he invited to the feasts. Every prosperous household would have had the place at the gate for the beggar, every servant would have known when and how to dispense the crumbs. Duty is done but no more. Only the dogs are said to do something more. When they have wounds themselves, they lick them as a cure. They do for the sick Lazarus just what they do for themselves. The same cannot be said of the rich man and the servants. They are prepared to do far less.

After the judgment, the rich man, who has died at the same time as the beggar, finds himself in the place of torment. There is no evidence in the parable that he is a wicked person. He seems more likely to be ordinary, just like everyone else around him, but fortunate. It is sometimes said that no one can make money and be honest at the same time. He may, along these lines, be too rich to be a good character. At the same time he is not represented making hard bargains, only enjoying what he has. According to the conventions of his time and his status he is not blameworthy. He keeps the rules, the beggar gets his crumbs, but he is devoid of higher aims. He does not think of using his money for the benefit of anyone but himself, and he is content with his pleasures. He has no thought for the morrow. He is sincerely attached to his family, thinking of his brothers when he is parted from them by death. They may well have forgotten him when the proper funeral ceremonies are over and done. It is particularly said in the parable that he was buried, suggesting a funeral in fine style according to his means, while of the beggar it is only said that the angels came to fetch his soul. The departure of a soul at death is in fact a double event. The friends here take farewell, the angels welcome him as someone new born. It would seem in the parable that there is a discrepancy. The rich man has only the notable leave-taking but the beggar the warm reception by the angels.

They indeed cannot do much with Dives who comes into the place of torment. How and why, when he seems so ordinary? His torment is thirst and the heat of flames. He has been a person who followed his own bent, doing what he liked because he could afford it. He has fostered in his soul tastes, longings and lusts, which he could satisfy while he was in the body. But without it he has no means of satisfaction, while the soul nevertheless feels and desires as it was accustomed to do. The thirst remains while the means of quenching it has gone. Conditions in the body can cause longings in the soul which, if they have never been restrained or overcome, can bring torment in the life after death. The greatest of all longings is that for the lost body itself. Even souls of composed character are liable to suffer for a period from torment of this kind. During the years of life here the soul becomes accustomed to having a body. It is the soul's original private house. It gives protection from too much experience, from over-much emotion and will coming from other people. It allows the soul to withdraw at will into his own inner world. Likewise it gives the means of having the experiences which the soul wants, of satisfying wishes and providing a sense of well-being.

'Oh, my body,' says the soul in longing for what is lost. 'You gave me shelter and the pleasure of experience. Above all you gave the chance to be myself. How shall I fare without you?' It is easy to see that Dives is not in the least prepared to lose the body, while Lazarus, who has been sick and hungry, welcomes the release from suffering. His soul departs easily, there being nothing to which he would cling.

The thirst of the soul in the first part of the life after death gradually exhausts itself. In the flames of longing the soul is purified of earthbound wishes. The rich man will not always be in torment. He is already emerging from the natural egotism of his nature when he begins to think of the danger of his brothers. Lazarus has so little to overcome that he has long passed into the care of Abraham, into which the rich man will come when his purification is complete. He can already see Abraham and talk to him from afar, although the replies are without comfort. Abraham's words seem to say that for every pleasure there will one day be pain and for every pain pleasure. A process of justice is at work in the world-order into which we enter at death. It is reflected in the old saying, 'the mills of God grind slowly but they grind exceeding small'. But the process is an inner one. It is not the pleasure that harms, but the unthinking selfishness that can possess the soul. It is not the pain that does good, but the effort to transform it into wisdom. Without pleasure there is too little strength. The beggar has had to lead a passive life of suffering, although he may have enjoyed the crumbs. But he has wisdom to take to the angels. The rich man shows energy before and after death, but he still has to learn wisdom.

Who is this beggar with the name of Lazarus? Every name in the Gospels is significant and many outstanding characters are nameless. In the parables only this beggar has a name and it means 'God has aided'. The name is also that of the brother of Mary and Martha dwelling in Bethany. He it is who fell sick and died, but was called from the grave by Christ with the words, 'Lazarus, come out.' This Lazarus had a title given to no one but himself in the Gospels. When he fell sick a message was sent to Jesus Christ: 'He whom you love is ill.' In the last chapter of St John's Gospel its author is spoken of as the one whom Jesus loved. The title links together Lazarus, who rose again, with the Evangelist and the apostle called John. Being reborn he came into a new name, for how could he have the old one when he had become a new person?

The expression 'whom Jesus loved' is a phrase, like some others in the Gospels, taken from the rites of the old mysteries, just as the manner of Lazarus' death and rising again followed their pattern. He was the neophyte or candidate for initiation and Christ the hierophant who presided and called his soul back to earth. The event was both old and new, an old pattern filled by Christ with a new purpose. Lazarus gave his life into the hands of his master and received it back again from him. Of such stuff was the love made that was between them. Only he among those who were around Jesus Christ was capable of that devotion which could be answered by the love which the hierophant would give to the closest disciple.

What link can there be between the beggar of the parable in St Luke's Gospel and the Lazarus who became the evangelist John? Why are they called by the same name? There may be many answers to this question, and what follows is only one among them. The parable of Dives and Lazarus was told within

87

a dispute between Christ Jesus and a group of Pharisees. They scoffed at him because they feared his stern saying: 'You cannot serve God and mammon.' He answered by warning them how great and decisive for the future was his own appearance on earth (Luke 16:16). 'The Law and the prophets were until John, since that time the kingdom of God is preached, and every man presseth into it.' But, he added, not the smallest part of the Law would fail, using the parable as illustration. The story seems just to say that justice is done. The rich man suffers and the poor one is comforted. As there was a great gap between their lot on earth, which they made no attempt to cross, so after death there is a great gulf between them which cannot be crossed.

When Abraham is asked by Dives to send the dead Lazarus back to earth to warn his brothers, he replies that they already have Moses and the prophets. Dives answers that this is not enough, they will repent only if someone goes to them from the dead. Abraham refuses the proposition and the story ends abruptly. He, throughout the conversation, represents justice. The rich man does not oppose the principle, nor deny that he suffers justly. But he makes two requests that introduce a theme of a new kind. He first asks for an act of grace for himself, that Lazarus shall come to him and touch his burning tongue with a cool finger. He then asks for a much greater act of grace for the sake of his brothers. The two requests point to a fact of human history. The Law had not ceased to be right, nor divine justice to prevail. Nevertheless human souls were falling deeper into the corruption of evil. Dives has known and kept the commandments but they have not saved him, an ordinary, stupid person of his time, from living in a way that has destroyed his soul. Moses and the prophets could not be wrong, but their influence is not strong enough to rescue the five brothers from making their own destruction. The Law has failed to save mankind.

Dives, in the pain of his experiences after death, becomes prophetic. He asks for new forces of the spirit to help mankind, and he names them. They are grace and the power to master death. Father Abraham cannot bestow them, seeming not even to understand them. Lazarus meanwhile is aware of what is being said, just as on earth he observed the comings and goings at the rich man's gate and he is still only an onlooker. Throughout the story, on both sides of the gate of death, he says nothing and does nothing. He suffers, he is comforted, he accepts and he is aware. He has a mind of his own but no will of his own. Dives, for all his thoughtlessness at first, is the active one, waking up in his pain to a new, far-sighted outlook, rousing himself to ask and ask again. Both he and Lazarus represent what had become of mankind in the long epochs of history before the turning-point of Christ's coming. Before and after death, Dives has had will, but no wisdom. Lazarus has wisdom, but no will. He has become a helpless beggar through the effect of being aware of his true spiritual human nature, but being unable to unfold or defend it on earth. The rich man thrives as long as he can remain happily unaware. Dives and Lazarus are in fact two halves of the same person. They are 'Mansoul', the one still linked with the worlds of spirit and alive in his thinking, the other dead to all but material interests and alive in his will. The interference of evil has made a split person of man.

The parable ends in an unsolved dilemma. Father Abraham is quite helpless, for he understands only the simple operation of justice, reward and punishment. There would be a tragic outcome to the story if the beggar were not called by the name of Lazarus. The dilemma is solved not in Luke's Gospel but in John's, not in a parable but in an event. He whom Jesus loved fell sick because he bore in himself the sickness of all mankind. He felt as his own the infirmity caused in human nature by the interference of evil. He died, for by then, in his age of history, mankind was exhausted of the forces that make for the future. He was raised by Christ Jesus to new life on earth, endowed with the forces of the spirit through which mankind continues to go on through evolution. He had died and was born again in and from the grace of Christ. He it was in whom the first stage of man's resurrection could be accomplished. In him the split between Dives and Lazarus, between will and thinking, between the spirit-filled and the earth-born, was healed. The true self had been born within him as he emerged from the grip of death, standing upright even while still wrapped in the grave-clothes.

How could this be? Martha heard the answer while Lazarus still lay in the grave: 'I am the resurrection and the life.' Within the picture of the parable these words would read like this: 'I am he who answers the prayer of Dives in torment after death. I give the grace, I bring the power to master the forces of death. Through my resurrection, Mansoul shall rise again.'

The figure of Lazarus coming out of the tomb has been painted often in the past in the likeness of a chrysalis from which a butterfly is about to emerge. The Lazarus of the parable is like someone wrapped away in a story not yet ready to be part of a real event. The Lazarus of history in St John's Gospel has emerged to offer himself to Christ for the performing of the new mystery of death and life. Man cannot find himself again through the Law and the prophets. He must press into the kingdom of God preached by John. Who was the first to go through death and resurrection into the kingdom but Lazarus, stepping out of a parable into history?

The Labourers
in the Vineyard

Emerson once said that every man is as lazy as he dares to be! But can the laziest of us really accept this dictum altogether, even if it is true from time to time? What of those hours when, weariness and disinclination no longer impeding, we forget everything but the purpose in hand? We have forgotten to be lazy, to argue the point of worthwhileness. For it is enthusiasm that carries us forward, the warm drive of the heart compelling the reluctant will. What seemed quite impossible is suddenly feasible, has happened before we know. Enthusiasm has consumed our inertia and our doubts, lifting us over the hindrances. The outer situation need not have changed but the inner one has triumphed. The mood of doing nothing is heavy and damp, soothing in its effortlessness but soon sinking under the weight of boredom. The mood of enthusiasm is fiery and stimulating and, overreaching itself, can be consumed in its own fire. The argument between the two would be like a dispute between water and fire. It would never be settled because, in spite of all preference, both are equally necessary. The person who does not know how to be lazy is always on tenterhooks. The one who cannot be kindled to enthusiasm is a wet blanket.

Matthew 20:1–16

> *'The kingdom of the heavens is like a human being, a*
> *master of his house, who went out early in the morning*

91

*to hire workers for his vineyard. After agreeing with the
workmen on a wage of a denarius a day, he sent them into
the vineyard. About the third hour he went out and saw
other workmen standing idle in the market place, and he
said to them, "You, too, go into the vineyard, and I will
give you a fair wage." And they went. And about the sixth
and the ninth hour he went and did the same. When he
went out about the eleventh hour he saw yet others standing
there; and he said to them, "Why do you stand here idle all
day?" They said, "Because no one has hired us." He said,
"You, too, go into the vineyard." And when the evening
came, the master of the vineyard said to his steward, "Call
the workmen and give them their wages; begin with the last,
then the others until you come to the first." So those who
had been hired about the eleventh hour came forward, and
each of them received a denarius. When it was the turn of
the first, they thought they would receive more. But they, too,
received a denarius each. They took it, but they grumbled at
the master of the house and said, "They came last and have
only worked one hour, yet you have made them equal to
us who have borne the burden and the heat the whole day
long." Then he said to one of them, "Friend, I am not doing
you an injustice. Did we not agree on a wage of a denarius?
Take what belongs to you and go. I wish to give to these last
as I give to you. Am I not free to do as I wish with what
belongs to me? Do you give me an evil look because I am
good? Thus the last will be first, and the first last".'*

The parable of the labourers in the vineyard is about working
and waiting. Like all of its kind, it is a story told with no
explanations. The picture is intended to explain itself, which it
will do only in response to hard thinking. There is no kind of story
so deceptive at first sight as one of the parables in the Gospels.
The picture is easy to recognise, since it is taken from a situation
well known in ordinary life. The plot is a straightforward piece of

drama. Yet it never quite means what one would easily expect. The more thought that is given to it, the more riddles it reveals. This is in fact only to be expected, for the parables are not the product of a human mind but of the God-filled mind of Christ himself. The wonder is that he could use the language of earthly life in a form simple in itself to convey ideas of divine proportions. He not only told the stories himself. He knew them, thought them and worded them, fashioning them into a special gift from the mind of God to the minds of men on earth.

That people work is apparently taken for granted in the parable under consideration. It is the story of the owner of an estate, who needed extra casual labour in his vineyard. No words are wasted in the parable on facts that every listener must have known. It does not say that the time had come to gather in the harvest but this clearly must be meant. Only at that season would a large number of extra hands be required for a job needing less skill than the cultivation of the vines at an earlier season. The owner, one would imagine, was concerned to get in the harvest of grapes quickly, as they had all ripened. To till a vineyard is an occupation filling the whole round of the year. But there is only one harvest, on which all the wealth of the vine-grower depends. There was much-needed work to be done in the vineyard of the parable and the owner looked for workers. The situation was simple: there was work to be done. No one said, 'Why work at all?' for the job that needed doing spoke for itself. Those who wanted jobs foregathered in the marketplace, the hub of affairs in the town or village. The owner went there early in the morning, when it grew light, and hired a number of those who offered themselves. No figure is given. He was careful to make a contract about payment. Each labourer was to receive a single denarius. The work began.

The owner, after three hours had passed, needed more workers. Again he went to the marketplace and hired others. This time there was no contract. The men were promised what would be right for less than a whole day's work. They went to join the first group at the job. The owner, however, after another three hours, went to the marketplace again and hired another group of workers, also leaving the amount of the wage uncertain. He did the same once more three hours later. The story has become more mystifying. Was he a bad manager that he could not calculate how much work was to be done and how many workers would be required? Surely he could look over his vineyard and estimate the yield of grapes to be gathered. Or, if he miscalculated the first time, he would not continue to do so at intervals. Or did the first labourers turn out to be less capable than they had looked to be and so needed reinforcements? But this too would not happen over and over again. The story shows a shift of emphasis as it continues. It starts with a vine-grower concerned for his harvest but it develops to the point at which he seems to have more concern for the fate of the workers than the vines.

The climax of the change comes when the owner sets out on his last journey to the marketplace. It was then the eleventh hour of a twelve-hour working day, lasting it would seem from sunrise to sunset. But by whom could the workmen have expected to be hired so late in the day? What was their mood? Why were they still abroad? The employer asked why they still stood idle and they replied that they had not been hired. But they were still waiting. He sent them to join the others in the vineyard for the final hour's work but without a contract. But why? What use would they be? If a realistic view is taken of what happens when there is a job to be done by a whole group of people at once, the arrangement seems less strange. If instead of calculating hours of work by statistics, as if each hour and the amount of work done in it were the same, the comparison is made with the train of events when someone gives a party for his friends, the behaviour of the vine-grower shows more sense. The labourers who began work early in the morning bore, as they said themselves later, 'the burden and the heat of the day'. They tired as the hours wore on. The newcomers could take over with new energy. In any party among friends, those who have made the preparations and done the work beforehand are happy if others come to lend a hand after it has begun.

The after-taste of the affair, the comments passed later, are affected by how much help has been offered with the clearing-up. Indeed, the resolve to give another party one day may well depend on how many extra helpers joined in during the last hour. So, in the parable, those who went in at the eleventh hour, after waiting so long, may well have been just those through whose efforts the vineyard was finally cleared of grapes before the day's end. It is the custom nowadays for employers to reckon by hours and output, without allowing for the quality of the work done or the variations of stress under which the workers labour. The arithmetic is simpler but the realities often lie outside such calculations. The history of strikes would produce many examples to this effect. If a private enterprise, based entirely on human relationships, is considered, like the giving of a party, the realities show up more clearly.

The question might be put whether the vine-grower of the parable, instead of being judged odd, was not in fact farsighted, even from the point of view that would apply within industry and commerce. Clearly, there must have been more people waiting in the marketplace in the early hours of the day than he offered to employ. He could have taken a somewhat larger number to work all day in the vineyard and saved himself further journeys to hire help. In fact many more people went to work for short hours than would have been strictly necessary. Was his method inefficient? From the point of view of getting the harvest gathered in the day, it would very likely have been more efficient. The quality of the work done must have been higher. So many labourers were glad to be called in, to have the opportunity to work. Those who came in at intervals during the day had fresh energy, since they had not yet been to work. The interest among the workers in each other was stimulated by new arrivals. Their concern for the job was kept alive and their wish to complete it renewed. What the vine-grower lost in time taken to visit the marketplace was compensated by the fresh interest in the outlook of the labourers. He would have a lively, willing team, some weary but experienced, others new to the job but fresh. They would be one with him in the determination to get the job well and truly finished.

The trend of the owner's behaviour, as the story advances, shows as much if not more interest in the labourers as in the clearing of the vineyard. His method of employment might well have been quite satisfactory. Nevertheless, he himself seems to have been very much concerned that those waiting in the marketplace should have the opportunity to work. His questions were not about how much they would be able and willing to do for his undertaking, but about their situation as unemployed. The picture is repeated on each of his visits to the marketplace of people standing idle who should be busy. His concern for their idleness grew as the day passed and came to a climax at the eleventh hour. Was he anxious for them because they were not earning the wage for the day, upon which the livelihood of themselves and their families depended?

Under the social conditions, which are implied in the Gospels, poorer people probably lived from day to day, as they do still in many parts of the world. No wage for a day would mean no food or very little. Almsgiving is mentioned as the duty of a good-living householder who is well enough off to have stores of food and clothing under his roof. Nowadays we are accustomed to count wealth in terms of money, but earlier a man's treasure consisted of actual goods. There being no other kind of public welfare, it was a duty to relieve the need of poorer neighbours. The rich had stores, the poor existed from hand to mouth. The rich could survive in times of trouble, the poor went under at once. When Christ sent out his disciples two by two to preach and to heal, he recommended to them the way of life of the poor. They were to take nothing but what they were using at the time. 'Carry no purse, nor bag, nor sandals' (Luke 10:4). They were to live on hospitality. 'Remain in the same house, eating and drinking what they provide.' They were to accept their livelihood from the rich. They were not therefore to behave like beggars, taking what they could get. The hospitality would be their due, because of what they themselves would have to offer. They were to comport themselves like 'labourers worthy of their hire'. They were to live from day to day.

Under such conditions, the vine-grower would, as a man of substance, have had the same duties of alms-giving and hospitality as others like him. He would not have been required to employ the labourers in order that they and their families could eat. He could have fed them from his own table. Nor is any mention made in the parable of hunger for food and money. The owner was concerned and anxious for their idleness. Not to be given the opportunity to work was the wrong done to them from his point of view. They had been deprived, not in the first place of a wage but of the chance to work, to make their contribution. Whatever may be felt nowadays about the joys of idleness when it does not involve want, the parable has something quite other to say. Idleness is a tragic condition. It puts people in the position of being the unwanted, superfluous ones. Their human status is reduced because they exist but they are prevented from doing. Idleness is a form of imprisonment in one's self. It is to be observed that it is only enjoyed by those who could, if they wished, emerge into activity. The sick, the very old, the unemployed often long to escape from it and find their human worth in being useful somehow to someone.

If this is so, why did the vine-grower not take pity on all those standing about in the marketplace much earlier in the day and for their own sake employ them all? That would have meant turning their chance to work into a charity. An illusion would have had to have been produced that their work was needed when in reality it was not. It would have been unsatisfactory all round. In fact they were not finally condemned to idleness but they had to wait. Waiting, they had to overcome the temptation to give up and disappear from the marketplace in despair. What endurance it must have meant that those employed at the eleventh hour were still waiting when their chance came! They suffered every phase of the pain of enforced idleness but they had learnt to wait. Idleness is not the only evil. Overbusyness is its opposite. It can produce a bustle of activity without a purpose, in which doing something becomes an end in itself. Overbusy people can be afraid of being still and waiting. They too are imprisoned, not within themselves but outside themselves, shut up in all that they are doing and dare not leave. It is as valuable to be able to wait positively as to work productively. The true human being should be equally able to work and to wait. The balance is shown very fairly in the behaviour in the parable of the owner. He accepted the fact that some must wait until they were needed while others worked. But he handled his affairs so that all in due time might contribute to the real progress of the work.

A motto coined by the poet William Blake reads, 'Rest before labour'. He was speaking of labour in its highest form as the act of creation. He perceived that the creative pause is necessary to prepare the act itself, that waiting is in truth the gathering of strength for working. When the force is exhausted, there will be another pause, not for weariness but for fresh preparation. If this is true of the labour of the artist, does this hold good for all work? What is the true secret of work?

Rudolf Steiner in his spiritual researches found that the old traditions about the zodiac were derived from realities. There is interaction between the influences of the stars and human existence on earth. The zodiac, the belt of constellations encircling the earth, can be watched as it moves through the round of the year. The invisible influences can be traced by their effects on the pattern of human existence. When a human soul enters into the world of earth and lives in a body, the forces that form the constitution will be found to be related to the working of the twelve signs.

For instance, the soul needs to keep contact with the universe, the place of its origin, to save itself from becoming earthbound. The soul looks back by virtue of the forces that proceed from the sign of Aries. The universe gives the power of movement to the soul, while the earth provides inertia. The sign of Taurus lets flow the forces that bring movement. But the two following signs, Gemini and Cancer, have an opposite effect. They inspire the forces that impel the soul to take hold of its separate existence in the body. Each of the twelve signs radiate into the human constitution on earth but the four that send their influences into the limbs do not finish their work in the functions of the body. A gap is left open in the twelvefold circle of forces, not in the headpiece nor in the chest but in the constitution of the limbs. They have, therefore, a great range of free movement. They complete in action what was left incomplete in their form and function. We can, for instance, alter our mode of breathing only so far as the functions of lungs and chest allow. There are restrictions in this part of the body unknown in legs and feet, arms and hands. They are capable of activities so various that no one person has the energy or skill to master them all. The forces of the signs Sagittarius, Capricorn, Aquarius and Pisces work into their power of action.

The four original kinds of work to which people first turned in earliest history and which are continued today are inventions of the limbs. That is to say, neither reason nor pressure of circumstances produced them but the forces of the universe flowing through the limbs. The hunter, the herdsman, the tiller of the soil and the merchant work out of the original human instinct to take hold of and use what nature had to offer. By their work they fashion the human way of life on earth. No earthly experience has taught human beings how to do this. They are inspired by the forces which they brought with them from the universe at birth. They do not accept their surroundings. They have the urge to alter, to exchange, to add and to invent. The hunter bestirs himself to chase and to take. The herdsman gathers the animals to himself, but changes their nature in part by domesticating them for his use. When the soil is tilled, an even greater change is made in the state of nature. The fields are made to yield harvests that are taken away from the life of the land to feed humankind. The merchant moves goods from place to place, from household to household. His work enables people to withdraw from the world of nature into their own separate existence in villages and towns. Man has to work to make a place for himself in the world of the earth.

That people work is taken for granted in the parables because the pattern of existence on earth has to be completed by human energy and skill. Man finishes the unfinished work of creation by his labour. He works therefore to gain what he needs. Just this is represented in the parable by wages or earnings. All the labourers were paid at the day's end as a matter of course. The strange note comes in when we hear how they were paid. A queue was formed to pass the steward who had to hand out the money. But those came first at the head who had last come to work and had done the shortest stint. Then came those who were called in immediately before them and so on until at the tail end those followed who had started at daybreak and worked through noon until sunset. Those who had waited were taken before those who had worked. The first labourers had had a contract for a denarius for the day. The others had none. But they each received the same coin. In spite of the contract, those who had laboured all day expected more when they saw the pay-out. When they did not receive more, there was trouble. A spokesman put himself forward to complain. The owner could and did prove him wrong, because he had accepted a contract which had in fact been honoured.

Each labourer had similar needs and took home the same money. This is a method of payment as valid as the usual one of paying for hours spent or the amount produced. It already operates under some circumstances nowadays. It can really happen that people are paid not to work as they might otherwise be paid to work. The practice of paying pensions and children's allowances is the result of recognizing the needs of those who cannot give their work for wages. The strange practice of the vine-grower could be understood in the same sense. Whatever the appearances, it is not really so that people are paid for their work. They may earn a living at a job but they work away at many other things without counting the cost. Or perhaps it should be said that the cost cannot be counted. The price of a picture, the value of a lesson, the fee of a musician, the salary of a nurse – who can calculate such work in terms of money? Yet all such workers need a livelihood that they may continue to work.

The vine-grower, faced with the man who complained, did not take his stand only on the contract. He spoke of his own will and purpose, which should have become understandable to the labourers who had been all day on the job. At the opening of the parable it is said that the owner represents the kingdom of heaven. What he has undertaken cannot be understood without seeing the story in terms of evolution in the widest sense. The vineyard is the earth and the labourers are human souls sent to work there by God himself. A harvest is to be gathered, for God has not undertaken the creation of human beings, the setting up of a world in which they can unfold independently, just to provide them with experience. They are meant to work, to become productive not for their own sakes but in order to give to the universe a harvest in return for the great cosmic forces that have been given to them. What is needed in the universe can only be grown and produced on earth. The director of the undertaking is God. He looks on the evolution of the human being on earth as significant for his divine purpose. Man, who will not himself consume the harvest for which he has laboured, must receive a reward for his work. There is a double nature to work. On the one hand, we look for its results. On the other, we observe that workers themselves become different because of what they have done. They learn, mature, acquire skill and most of all come nearer to themselves because of what they have done.

The payment of the labourers was made by means of a single coin, of which each received one. It belonged to him only, in contrast to the produce of his labour, which was at the disposal of the owner for wider purposes. Each has made his contribution to the great undertaking, putting his effort into it as far as he had been given the chance for the benefit of the whole. He then took with him his coin, round, complete in itself, the picture of wholeness. Now he had something to work with for himself. At the day's beginning he had nothing. He could only wait and offer his labour. At the day's end he was in possession of something for which he was responsible and could use in his own way. Experience of life goes to show that people often come to themselves through owning something or taking on a responsibility. Each workman in the parable had his coin, but it was not something in itself; it represented a value of another kind. It stood for what the kingdom of heaven intended each human soul to gain from the undertaking, self-possession in the sense of selfhood realised from within. Other possessions may help to develop the character but the ultimate aim will be to possess one's own will in inner freedom.

At the beginning of the day the labourers were entirely dependent on the owner. At the end the coin of self-possession was put into their hands. For this reason each workman received the same, whether he had worked many or few hours. All were willing to work the whole day, but some had to wait. At long last all were given the opportunity to earn in God's great undertaking the coin of true wholeness, of selfhood in the spirit. But what had happened to the grumblers that they complained? They had missed the point. At the end of the day's work they were still thinking of themselves as employees who could go on strike regardless of the welfare of the undertaking. Theirs was the tragic experience of having worked hard for a purpose which they had not understood. By concentrating so narrowly upon their own profit, they missed realizing their part within the whole. When they should have become able to think like partners, they were still arguing like strikers.

From the point of view of one moment in time, there are great inequalities in life. Some individuals seem to go ahead, to be active, to achieve. Others seem destined to much waiting about and looking on. Among the nations and peoples it is the same. Some are in the forefront of history, some well behind, some finished, others not yet begun. According to the parable, they will all be called to their due place in the great undertaking although it may be at the ninth or the eleventh hour. To the mind of the employee who sees only the present moment, it is most unfair. To the mind of the partner who has some insight into the whole, who looks back into the past and on into the future, no other method of work seems possible.

Where is Christ himself within the picture of the parable? He is the paymaster, who hands the coin of great meaning to each of the labourers. When he does so, the nature of work is given a new significance. At the beginning man was made unfinished and must work for a living in the alien world of earth. Now work itself also has a purpose for the future. This world is to be transformed by human activity into another condition. The world's ending is being prepared. Nature, left to herself, does not produce vineyards. They require continual cultivation under conditions that make the work very hard. Left to grow wild they are useless. The grapes from the vines come to their greatest use when they are put through various processes, all involving human labour.

When the earth is compared to a vineyard, of which God is the owner, as it is in this parable, it implies that he is looking towards the future. The earth as she is by nature is his creation. But he is not shown in his concern for what he has created, but for that part of the earth which is changed by human effort. The harvest which he is intent on gathering is produced when human work and the life of nature combine. Without people who change ground into fields, there would be no harvest gathered into the kingdom of heaven for the sake of the universe. Without the presence of Christ there would be no understanding in human souls for their part in the undertaking and its purpose. They could be labourers and servants of God. But when they receive the coin of selfhood, they are servants only if they wish to be. They have the means of becoming partners. Their work has changed them and they will transform the world.

The King's Invitation

During earlier epochs, ordinary people were directed by the will of the gods. In the later ones they were led by kings and princes. Still later great men governed them. Now people have to make their own fate. But how are they going to make good as ordinary people?

Among the parables in the Gospels told by Jesus Christ, one, in the Gospel of St Matthew, speaks of just this dilemma of history. The parables, having come as they all have from the mind of Christ himself, are all directed in various ways to one main idea. They speak of human evolution on earth as it is seen by God in the divine world. It is no wonder that the most modern of dilemmas is found pictured among them. It represents an important crisis in the making of history as a whole.

Matthew 22:1–14

And Jesus continued to speak in parables to them: 'The kingdom of the heavens is like a human being, a king, who prepared a marriage feast for his son. And he sent out his servants to call the guests who had been invited to the marriage, but they would not come. Then he again sent out other servants and said, "Say to those who have been invited, see, I have prepared my banquet, the oxen and the other fatted beasts have been slaughtered; everything is ready. Come to the wedding." But they disregarded it and

went off, one to his field, another to his business. The others
took hold of the servants, maltreated them and killed them.
Then the king grew angry; he sent out his army, destroyed
the murderers and set fire to their town. Then he said to
his servants, "Although the marriage feast is prepared,
the guests have not proved themselves worthy of it. Now
therefore go to the remotest roads and invite to the wedding
whoever you find." And the servants went into the streets
and gathered all whom they found, bad and good. And the
wedding hall was filled with guests. Then the king came in
to see the guests, and among them he noticed a man who
was not dressed in the wedding garment. And he said to
him, "My friend, how did you get in here, since you are
not wearing a wedding garment?" And he was speechless.
Then the king said to the servants, "Bind him hand and
foot and cast him out into the darkness of external existence
where human beings live, lamenting and gnashing their
teeth." For the call goes to many, yet only a few make
themselves real bearers of higher life.'

This parable, like many others, seems to be a story about a
human situation. A wedding has been arranged. The invitations
are to be sent out by the father of the bridegroom, unlike the
custom of today. But the situation does not develop within the
parable in the way that would be expected. The invitations do not
lead on to the story of the marriage itself. The guests are seen and
described, but not the bride and the bridegroom. Has the most
important part been left out? Such a question can open up the
parable's deeper meaning.

This one, like most other parables, opens with the words 'The
kingdom of the heavens is like ...' In other words, God in this
picture is to be represented by a king who made a marriage for his
son. The story begins with the issuing of invitations. God invites,
but whom? The guests, it seems, are to be human ones, who are
living on earth. Nothing is said of others of whom it would be

natural to think first – angels, archangels and all the company of heaven or the great and glorious dead who stand before the throne. Only guests concerned with the history made on earth are described. It is not said in particular who they are, but they are not just nobodies, because they are invited when others are not. Who are those in this world who have the right to receive first the invitation from God? Except that they are busy people, who refuse to come, little is said of them. More can be learnt by looking at what is said about the servants. It is characteristic of the parables as a whole that important parts in the stories are given to servants. And indeed those who give service have a great influence in any situation in ordinary life. The patient depends on the nurse, the passengers on the driver, the diners on the cook. The style of the parables is realistic.

The king's invitation is carried by servants twice to the same people and once to others. In spite of the parable's sparse account of what happened, one point is stressed. The two first invitations are taken round by different sets of servants, although they go to the same guests. The second time it is said that 'other servants' are sent. At the first invitation the replies are all in the negative. At the second more detail is given. The king reminds the unwilling guests that the feast is prepared and they should come and eat it. What a strange host! No one has accepted the invitation but he seems to have continued preparing the food as if they would all come. The human situation is well known, when friends have been invited, preparations made and no one turns up. Few people to whom this has happened forget it in years. But at least the guests had not all refused beforehand. Only God could take straight refusals in such a manner.

In the account of the second invitation the guests are distinguished as to behaviour. Still no one accepts because everyone is preoccupied. Earthly affairs intervene to provide excuses: for some a farm, for others the market. Everyone is simply too busy making a success of his business, whether as producer or middleman. But there are exceptions. Some guests take the invitation much more seriously, opposing it and maltreating the servants who bring it. They are roused to violence by being bothered a second time. They turn against the king and his summons.

The first servants who were sent out return with sad news, but the second have to suffer – some even to die. Their wrongs are avenged later by the king's armies but their suffering has not been prevented. Who are these servants, of two kinds, some so badly treated? The guests are people with rights of their own to be the first invited by the king. Far back in the early stages of history as it is reckoned today, great kings ruled over tribes and nations of people. Their authority depended on their access to sources of divine inspiration not available to everyone. They were part priest and part king, without the distinction expected today. In the earliest times the great king-heroes claimed to be descended from the gods themselves. Some would tell of a divine father and a human mother and others of a goddess-mother and a human hero for father. This was a matter of pride for their descendants. Still earlier the gods themselves had walked on earth with men and women and been their leaders. Then they had begun to withdraw, the Greeks said to Mount Olympus while others spoke of other heavenly residences. The gods became visitors, met more often in dreams than in waking life, still ready to give inspiration and counsel but hard to contact. They could be sought in the shrines dedicated to them and called upon there through the priests, who knew and would observe the proper rites. In the Old Testament, a like story is told of Yahweh, who withdrew from Adam and Eve behind the closed gate of the Garden of Eden.

The first set of servants were sent out at the time of history during which the lesser gods, in Christian terms archangels and angels, brought tidings of the will of God to men. The very mention in the parable that the second set of servants is different from the first points to two stages in the history of man's relationship to the spiritual world. As long as divine beings came and went as messengers, the invitation could be refused but the invited guests had no power over the servants. At the same time certain people in the human community became more important than the rest. It was held to be quite impossible for affairs on earth to be conducted rightly without directions from the divine world. As in the course of time the gods withdrew further and further off, so it became ever more difficult to get divine answers to human questions.

The famous holy places in the ancient world where the oracles could be consulted became international centres of power. Those who presided over them acquired immense influence. It is not hard to imagine how corruption could creep in. Powerful rulers could forestall the dictates supposedly coming from the gods and priests, could pull the strings behind the pronouncements made in the sanctuary. Those whose authority came from their position as mediators between gods and men turned from the king's messengers to make profit for themselves in the business of earthly affairs. Divine messengers came more and more rarely. But once, after they had ceased to come often, an archangel actually reached the earth, impelled by the importance of his message. Gabriel appeared to the priest Zacharias in the Temple to foretell the birth of John, the herald of the Messiah. He came a second time to the maiden Mary to announce the birth of Jesus, whose mother she was to be through the working of the Holy Spirit.

The second set of servants sent at a later time in history were human. They became the messengers of God because they were receptive to his inspirations at a time when the gods had withdrawn. They appeared on the stage of history as leaders, lawgivers and prophets. They like the first were not always heard. Many were opposed and even martyred. Such messengers are described in the Old Testament and the most impressive is Elijah.

Elijah delivered his messages with the saying, 'Thus says the Lord ...' He never spoke his own mind but gave only his message. He lived on two levels of consciousness: the ordinary one, of which little is said in his story, and the inspired one that is described in the pictures of his nearly magical adventures. As a messenger he was indomitable, speaking without fear or favour. As a person he was vulnerable. Feared by the king, hated by the queen, he became a runaway in wild places. He paid the price of his service as a messenger of the Lord by going in fear of his life. At the peak of his loneliness and despair, he received a message of a different nature from those that had come to him before. It was not meant for the people of his time but for those of many generations later. In a cave on the holy mountain, he had a meeting with the Lord himself, whose messenger he had been. He heard what had never been heard before – the still small voice, which was God speaking within his very heart. God had spoken to man until that hour from without, giving commands, sending messages. Now he began to speak within the shrine of the human heart. The messenger found that the message had become part of himself.

When the invitation had been rejected by the chosen guests the servants were sent out a third time. The king had made ready the wedding; now guests are invited without distinction of persons. All who are going about the business of ordinary life are to be brought in from the thoroughfares. The servants are said to collect both bad and good. The time has come for the 'common man' to receive the invitation which the leaders have rejected. Everyone accepts at once. The story would be simpler if it ended here but it does not. Something is required of the hastily gathered guests. They are required to wear garments suitable to the wedding feast. There is an often quoted oriental tradition that the host at a feast lends garments for the occasion to his guests. Whether or not such a custom is assumed in the parable, the stress is laid not on the problem of his acquiring a garment but on his being unwilling to wear one. To approach the meaning of the final scene in the drama, in which the unclothed guest is thrown out, it is necessary to ask the question about what the mysterious marriage means, which we never see clearly because the guests block the view.

The king, who is God, has arranged and prepared the marriage. His Son is the bridegroom. The picture of the divine marriage is found in the gospels recurrently and finally at its grandest at the end of the Book of Revelation. It signifies Christ coming to raise the spirit of man into the community of God in the universe. The bride is Mansoul whom the bridegroom calls to make herself ready to accept the union with himself. No wonder that the bride does not appear in the parable, for she is surely not yet prepared. The invitation to take part in the divine marriage is the call of God to human souls to receive a new revelation of the spirit. It comes not once but many times, through an experience from within, through an event from without, through a thought or a word. An answered prayer means that a guest has accepted an invitation. Did not the one who prayed invite the answer? This is not so, for the answer to the prayer is already there before it is uttered.

The invitation to pray is sent again and again from God. The Sacrament itself is the highest example of the call to human souls to go to meet the spiritual world in and through Christ. It is the holy union of the spirit of man with the Spirit of God. Today, when the Christian Eucharist has been reborn in the Act of Consecration of Man (as celebrated in the Christian Community) the divine invitation is sent once more, not to the chosen but to all and everyone. This is expressed in the custom that no one, friend or stranger, prepared or unprepared, is excluded from taking part. The celebrant offers the Communion from the altar steps. Those who wish to partake stand and approach ready to receive. The invitation is open without conditions, the responsibility for accepting lies with those who choose to take. They make one significant action out of their own will. They stand up and move forward, at the sign of invitation.

When, in the parable, the king has gathered his guests, he expects something of them. He has provided everything, the marriage ceremony and the feast. But one part, small in proportion to what is offered, is nevertheless required from those who come. Those who were first summoned were expected to leave their own concerns for a while and attend the wedding. The affairs of the king were on that occasion to supersede theirs. Those called from the thoroughfares of life, with no great concerns of their own, come willingly but are expected to be worthy guests nevertheless. They have to wear the right clothes and to behave correctly. When, in the last episode of the story, the king speaks to the guest who is not properly dressed, he asks him a question, 'My friend, how did you get in here?' The guest is speechless. He cannot face the host, answer a courteous question or behave in any sense as he should. Is the king expecting too much? Having called in all and sundry, having opened the mystery of the marriage to the common man, should he not then say, 'Nothing can now be expected, not clothing, speech or behaviour. Why cast out from the feast into the darkness outside a man from the street who just came in with the crowd?'

Behind the picture of the marriage is hidden the mystery of the great calling offered by God to man. He is called not to remain for all future time a creature of the world here but to become a member of the spiritual community of the universe. Through his experiences here, he can develop his humanity to its true higher stages. But he should not be identified always and only with the position, possessions and concerns that furnish the ordinary personality. There should be hours in life of high importance given up to divine affairs, when man accepts that he is called to be one of the sons of God. He should be concerned then, not with himself, but with the purposes of evolution. He should look ahead to the future that is already held for him in the hands of God. He is now a guest and onlooker because he is intended to become a partaker in the marriage itself. When the bride is made ready the spirit of man will be called by Christ, the bridegroom. The Father invites the guests, but the Son will invite the bride. Man becomes what he is to become on earth, but his ultimate, destined place is among the angels, archangels and all the company of heaven. He is prepared for his high destiny by being already now invited from time to time to be the guest of the divine king.

But what has this to do with the ordinary man in the street? It would seem from the parable that God, in earlier times of history, accepted that it would be too much to ask of him that he face the whole destiny of mankind. Certain leaders were chosen to undertake this for him. But they could not continue to do so. God himself then recognised that history must change and advance to the age of the common man. But when he sends the invitation far and wide, he is not resigned to ordinary people remaining ordinary. He summons them to the high calling earlier reserved for the chosen few. He is not prepared to accept the members of mankind just as they are. He shows them what they have to become when they accept the invitation. He does not lower the standard to suit the type of guest. All present must know that they are to take a proper part in that which concerns the whole evolution of mankind.

But does he throw out for good the useless among the guests? The place of outer darkness, of grief and pain, is spoken of in a number of parables. There is no evidence that it is meant to be understood as a hell to which human souls are condemned for ever. In the language of the parables, grief is taken to speak for itself; that is to say, to be an experience that awakens and chastens the soul. It brings insight where before there was soul-blindness. The rejected guest will have the chance to awaken to his own condition, to see where he has failed, to start learning what he has missed. The divine invitation is not only received once. The messengers are sent again and again. He who was thrown out will, should he accept the lesson of grief, have other chances to attend the feast, to speak, to dress and to behave as a true guest.

112

What is the secret of the wedding garment? The eternal soul of a person is clothed with the thoughts, feelings and intentions that become part of the personality. Character is the garment of the self. This is the most personal of all concerns, where we alone decide for ourselves what we shall become. Our interests, meeting the effects of experience, will form and shape us. The king in the parable is not willing to take from any of his guests this kind of responsibility for himself. If he would do so what then? He would deprive them of the high human calling, which is the meaning of the invitation. God calls people, not for what they are but for what they should become. No one is without the material for his wedding garment, because he receives from the life before birth, from the hands of the Great Ones of the universe, the forces of soul with which to cultivate his life of spirit in addition to managing his affairs on earth. But he it is who has to make use of them, to decide how far he remains a man in the street and how far he becomes a worthy guest at the king's feast.

We become that which we admire. This principle is the secret of the myths and legends, the statues and the holy pictures of the past. Now that the common man has taken over, what will become of him? Will he say, 'I am all right as I am, let history be cut down to my size'? Will he deprive himself of admiration for what is greater than himself? If he does so, he will become the derelict of evolution, for no one stands still. The phrase 'the age of the common man' means something when it implies that now it is he who receives the divine invitation. The foremost temptation of the great leaders in past ages was to become preoccupied with their own greatness. The chief temptation of common people is to neglect their wedding garment, to expect so much to be given to them that they do not ask of themselves that part which the divine king asks of them. In their dilemma, they have the help of the messengers who bring the invitation, if they will listen. They have been invited to the marriage at which the bridegroom is Christ. When they behold the Son in his truth, they look up to the vision of that which is beyond themselves. They know then why they are not all right as they are, why they should prepare themselves to dress, speak and act as proper guests at the marriage feast of the king.

The Wise and Foolish Virgins

The clock ticks time away: the moments are gone and do not return. What we say, what we do, our very existence flows away on time. This kind of experience could bring anyone to the point of losing his nerve, but an experience of another kind comes to the rescue. It is the confident assumption of everyone that when the sun sets at dusk it will rise again at dawn and a new day will begin. Time is expected to move in recurring rhythms – day following night, spring coming after winter. Our plans and doings are adjusted to such an assumption. This other experience of time can produce a sense of certainty, in contrast to the dread arising from the sensation of time flowing from the past into the present and away beyond.

There is still a third experience of time, through which the shocks, pleasant and unpleasant, arrive to disturb the patterns of life. When something unexpected happens, it comes out of the future. The unexpected is not always without causes in the past, although it is easy to be deceived into overlooking them. But there are genuine, unexpected events, and they arrive on the stream of time flowing from the future into the present. To this stream belong also our plans, aims and purposes. As long as they exist only in thought, they have not happened yet. We draw them down into the present, as we put them into action. But the unforeseen events arrive out of their own volition.

The present moment is in itself a mysterious thing, a meeting point between past and future, nothing in itself and yet everything. It is literally the only time that we can be said to have. It is our own, because we can do something with it. We can change and become something different in it. Thoughts are often turned towards the past in remembrance or to the future in hope and dread. The present moment is obscured and we lose sight of what we have, because of what we once had or what we might have.

Matthew 25:1–13

'Then the kingdom of the heavens will be like ten maidens who took their lamps and went out to meet the bridegroom. Five of them were dull of soul, five were alert and prudent. The foolish indeed took their lamps, but they forgot the oil. The sensible ones took flasks of oil for their lamps. Now, because the bridegroom was a long time coming, they all became tired and fell asleep. But in the middle of the night the call went up: See, the bridegroom is coming, go out to meet him! Then all the maidens rose and trimmed their lamps. And the foolish said to the prudent, "Give us some of your oil, for our lamps are going out." But the prudent said, "No, the oil would not be enough for us and for you as well. You had better go to the dealers and buy oil for yourselves." And while they were away, buying, the bridegroom came; and those who were ready to receive him went with him into the wedding hall, and the doors were closed.

'Afterwards the other maidens came also and said, "Lord, Lord, open to us!" But he replied, "I tell you once for all, I do not know you."

'So be alert of soul, since you do not know the day or the hour.'

The parable of the wise and foolish virgins is set within the problem of time. It speaks about what may be done with the three kinds of time. It begins after the usual manner of the parable with the phrase 'The kingdom of the heavens will be like ...' A parable is a likeness in story-form to which the clue is given in the opening words. To get at its meaning, it is important to start from the clue, observing it carefully. In the case of this parable, it can come as a shock to realise that the kingdom of heaven is not likened to the bridegroom, as would easily be expected, but to the ten maidens themselves. It is clearly said that the likeness applies to the whole group of ten, including the foolish ones equally with the wise. They were to be the bridesmaids at a wedding. Surely the most important people at a wedding are bride and groom. But they are put into the background of the story, while the front place is given to the bridesmaids. They had one function to perform, to light lamps when the bridegroom would appear.

Who were these maidens? They were collected in a group, which is emphasized by their number being ten. The figure twelve is used in the language of the Bible to represent the complete whole, of which the parts are individual and different. For instance, the twelve apostles were a group of separate people, each a type in himself, who together could represent humankind as a whole. In contrast, the figure ten means a crowd of undifferentiated people, who could be numbered off in units. The maidens were all alike, young girls who had not started to live out their separate destinies, who would as a group stand round the bride. The occasion was to be hers, when she would step out of undistinguished girlhood into her own particular life. They would provide the chorus in the background, while she had the solo part.

They were virgins, and that in the picture language of the Bible means that they were only halfway down to earth. Still enwrapped in the heavenly forces with which they had entered the world at birth, they had not yet become complete earthly personalities. In the religious life of earlier times, that condition was highly valued. Long before orders of nuns were founded in the Christian Church, there was an order of priestesses in Rome, the Vestal Virgins, who tended the eternal flame, kept burning in honour of the goddess. Among other ancient peoples similar customs prevailed. The dedicated virgins were kept apart, so that the forces belonging to the life before birth would live on in a certain group of the population for the welfare of the whole people. Why should the kingdom of heaven be represented in the picture of a group of girls in their green youth? A figure similar to those in the parable is to be found in a poem by William Blake called 'The Book of Thel'. The maiden Thel represents the human soul as she awakens to self-consciousness and asks the riddle of her own existence. The ten maidens are human souls, not as yet distinguished by a fully conscious selfhood , but filled by the substance of soul which they have had since birth. Such substance comes from the divine world with each soul as it incarnates.

The kingdom of heaven is identified with the maidens because of just this in their nature. They are heaven-born and only creatures of earth in part. In this sense the ten maidens are everybody. As a group they form 'Mansoul', to use an old English expression. The opening words of the parable could be paraphrased like this: the kingdom of heaven is like Mansoul just come down to earth. But five of the maidens were wise and five were foolish, half and half. The kingdom of heaven is likened to them all, both kinds included. The Greek word used in the original text where 'wise' is said in English means particularly a virtue of the mind, to be far-sighted, prudent and wakeful. The word for 'foolish' is the opposite, meaning dull, fatuous and sleepy of mind. In a modern conversation the wise maidens would be said to be 'all there' and the foolish to be 'dopey'. It is not a matter of saying that half were good and half were bad, but that half were awake in mind and half were not using their minds at all.

All the maidens were alike in knowing what was expected of them and being in agreement. They were preparing for a wedding and especially for the arrival of the bridegroom. They were all equipped with the necessary lamps. There was no shortage of oil. All that each maiden was required to do was to take the necessary oil and have it ready beforehand. Short as the parable is, several of its sentences are devoted to stressing the fact that there was no lack of oil to be obtained easily. Later on the foolish maidens found themselves going to buy it at midnight and they could do so. The shops were open, or at least their request was heard and answered. They had no arguments about the money to pay. Reading the parables requires special attention to what is said between the lines by implication as much as to the words used. One important point has been made in the telling without direct explanation. None could accumulate more oil than they could use themselves, nor could they store up supplies for longer periods. The oil was there for the having, but each had to take their own share. Provided she was awake to the situation, each maiden could have ready what she would need for the wedding.

Here the point has been reached where the story has departed from the logic of ordinary life. It would have been easy when the story was first told to picture the scene, because everyone would have known about a wedding ceremony. But suddenly the picture has been put out of the ordinary, because something of another kind had to be said. In ordinary life a person could store up oil if he could afford it. The maidens could not do so. Mysteriously, this was not possible, although day and night each of them could obtain oil in the shops for herself.

The secret of this part of the parable is connected with the streams of time flowing from the past into the present. The maidens were to be bridesmaids because of the kind of people they were and the position they were in, which allowed them to be invited. Their past had led up to this moment. The difference between the ten of them lay in the use that they had made of passing time. One half had been awake to what was required, trimming the lamps and filling them with oil. The other half must have said: why bother now, as there will be plenty of time for that when the lamps are actually needed. They were different in their awareness of the present moment. The foolish felt: the event itself will make us prepare, the present is still to come. The wise felt: the present can be used for making ready; it will be too late when the crisis is here. They were awake to the opportunity of the present, while the foolish went floating along on the stream of time, waiting.

There is also the time of recurring rhythms, in which each hour is the same length and each day is followed by the next. In relation to this time, all the maidens behaved in the same way. 'Now, because the bridegroom was a long time coming, they all became tired and fell asleep.' The old Greek language had more than one word for time. In the verb translated as 'was a long time in coming' is included the word *chronos*, which indicates time that passes on and on. It neither begins nor ends – it passes, In the period of waiting, which was simply time passing as usual, none of the maidens was awake in mind. This was said of them without reproach.

Here the parable has taken another surprise turn. Is not the very word for wisdom contradicted by the picture of the wise maidens in slumber? Recalling that at the beginning the kingdom of heaven was likened to the maidens, it is proper to the picture to say that this is sleep out of the ordinary. In a spiritual sense, a person occupied with outer affairs, with his mind on what he is doing, is asleep to the higher consciousness of the spiritual world, although it lives within him. In the routine of daily life he is asleep in this sense, but no blame is attached to him. The wrong element comes in when he assumes that this is all that is required of him and will not awaken to what comes on the other stream of time. In a higher sense one day is not just like another. A greater purpose is at work and, aware of this, the wise maidens prepared their lamps.

Their eyes were fixed on something to come, beyond their own experience. The bridegroom would appear in his own time – no one knew just when. His coming was not an event evolving logically out of the past. It was something out of the future coming into the situation provided by the past. It created an intense present moment of new beginning, a crisis. For this there is a particular word in the Greek of the Gospels, *kairos*. It is often indicated in the English by the phrase 'the time is at hand'. The stream from the future erupting into the time of *chronos* produces the crisis. The foolish maidens behaved towards all three kinds of time in the same way, hoping to be borne along by the events. When the crisis came, they were divided from their far-sighted companions by their own attitude. The coming of the bridegroom woke the wise maidens out of the sleep of ordinary life into awareness of the great occasion for which they had waited. It was the hour of their transfiguration. To the foolish ones, it was a disaster. Woken by the shock, they realised the need for oil. Helplessly they tried to save themselves through their companions. But each lamp was a strictly individual responsibility. They ran for oil but, when they had some, it was too late. The door was shut on the marriage and they were outside. They were defeated on a point of timing.

This parable has its own kind of logic. It promises a wedding but offers no sight of the bride but instead a shut door. The one who hears the story is not invited in at the climax by any description of what took place behind the door. If he knows for himself what marriage this was, he will be inside. If he does not know, the picture itself leaves him outside. It presents the threshold to the mystery and stops there. The centrepiece is the door, open to the wise and shut to the foolish, because the right of entry was given by the lighted lamp. Behind it was the mysterious bridegroom, whose voice could be heard but himself only seen by those who had entered. Who is he? He is Christ himself, coming out of the future into the situation made by the past, bringing the crisis of the new beginning. He came at midnight, when the past day had died away and the new one had not yet begun. He came to those who waited but could not know for what hour. He woke them from the sleep of earth, calling them to the marriage for which they had all been openly invited. But when the time came, it proved to be a mystery attended by the few and celebrated behind the closed door.

The marriage spoken of in the parable is an event that comes on the stream of time flowing from the future into the present. The bridegroom is a figure of promise. The marriage is not shown in the picture because it has not happened yet. Those who went behind the door could have revealed to them the mystery of man's future in the sense of Christ. But this is a powerful force in the history of the present. Anyone with a sense of purpose behaves accordingly now. So much the more does the Spirit of Christ move through earthly time with the divine sense of purpose which flows out from the Father in the heavens. How could the final aim be best described? Jesus Christ himself, who told the parable, chose the picture of the marriage, promised but not yet fulfilled. The bridegroom foreshadows the husband to be. Mansoul has been separated from the world of God by earth-existence. How can that which has been divided be brought together, be made one in the longing of conscious love?

The mystical marriage spoken of in the Gospels represents the culmination of human evolution according to the purpose of Christ. Mansoul was separated long ago by darkened consciousness of mind. The longing for the divine was never quite lost. The lighted lamp shines with the flame of the love kindled in the darkness. It lights up the mystery of the promised union, which will bring the long isolation to an end. The hidden bride, who is still not ready to be seen, will come forth as Mansoul transformed. The bridegroom will lead out the bride when the time for the marriage will have been reached. Then, in the words at the end of the Book of Revelation, the Spirit and the Bride will say: 'Come.' The last great invitation will be proclaimed. The door will be opened and never shut again.

At the centre of the parable is a prophecy. The bridegroom comes but the bride is being made ready by the maidens who have passed the door with their lamps. Each human soul who goes to meet Christ is helping to fulfil the future of all mankind, while being himself taken up into the mystery. In terms of the parable itself, the question arises when the bridegroom brings his light at midnight: surely the small flames in the lamps of the bridesmaids are unnecessary? But the parable seems to say that to see the greater light the soul needs the light of her own spiritual consciousness. She must have prepared it in advance. She cannot share it with others.

When the great illumination of Christ's presence dawns in the darkness of earthly life, it will be seen by those who have kindled their own particular inner light. They will qualify to be shown the mysteries of the future. In perceiving the meaning of man's evolution, they will find the deeper meaning of their personal existence.

Within the picture, the contrast between the maidens and the bridegroom speaks for itself of its significance. The maiden represents the human soul but not the whole human being. What is missing in the maiden comes to meet her in the bridegroom. The soul enters the world of earth at birth with many qualities. They are fulfilled when the true self unites with the soul. The individual being who can come to himself and call upon his own will is the true human being aware of the spirit within. It is Christ who brings the substance of the spirit to human souls. They have been fashioned by forces from the past, from the life before birth, but the self comes on the stream from the future. The marriage of the parable is a twofold mystery. It begins to take place now for any single soul who can light the lamp and is ready. It will be fulfilled for all humankind at the end of evolution, which is still far ahead. The mystery is always here, 'Be alert of soul.' And it is always ahead in the future, coming to meet us.

'I do not know you.' At the end of the parable, the bridegroom cried aloud these stern words of rejection to the unready maidens. Were these to be his last words to them, last and final? It might seem so, if the mystery of what is celebrated behind the shut door did not belong to the stream of time flowing from the future into the present. The future is still coming about. The marriage does not end here in the parable; it is just beginning. The bridegroom has not finished coming; he is in the process of coming still. The stern rejection could only be felt as a severe shock. The effect of shock is to awaken consciousness. The unready maidens had been asleep to the uses of the present for preparation. They could be spiritually asleep no longer, even though they had woken to the painful knowledge of being shut out. Their awakening was the new opportunity to make ready. Immediately after the cry 'I do not know you,' follow the words 'So be alert of soul.' Are they said by the same voice?

The parable is a story composed and told by Christ himself. The spirit behind the voice is the same. The arrangement of the two sentences one after the other comes from him. The style speaks as loudly as the words. The maidens, human souls of all kinds, may awaken and begin to watch in earnest at any time. Chronological time passes on from day to day. The hour of crisis can come at all seasons without warning. Each one has his own hour over which Christ watches. Each one must bring the lamp which only he can light. The door is opened and the door shuts. The past is not everything. The present is the time that belongs to each one of us for himself. But the present is made from the future in the meeting with the past. It is the hour like the one that has just gone. But it may be the hour of the bridegroom's coming.

The Parable of the Talents

'Do but consider what an excellent thing sleep is ... Who complains of want, of wounds, of cares, of great men's oppressions, of captivity, whilst he sleepeth? Beggars in their beds take as much pleasure as kings: can we therefore surfeit on this delicate Ambrosia?' Thus Thomas Dekker (1572–1632) wrote long ago, and anyone will agree with him today, when often enough he who can sleep is a king compared with him who begs for sleep in vain. Sleep has a charm like nothing else. It saves us from ourselves. Each day all people must be themselves, walk the streets to which they belong, because they are what they are. But when sleep begins, when the soul is unloosed from the body, the limits are transcended, the self emerges into the universe with all its vastness of space and time. The self seeks again the place of its origins, while the soul can gather in the fields of the stars its proper food. Sleep is a going home.

What do we not owe to sleep? Our companions in the world beyond the door of sleep are those of whom we lose sight when we are awake. Here we see the pattern of the stars. There we can watch the procession of the heavenly hierarchies. The different stars are like nameplates on the doors of the residents in the heavens. Behind them live and move the great ones to whose working we owe what we have and are. In sleep we go behind the door of their residences, for each one of us has a representative there, someone to introduce us. The angels are the least in the procession after ourselves but they are our helpers in the world too vast and vivid for our human consciousness. Each guardian angel can guide the soul of the sleeper who is under his care and lead him aright.

Sleep is the little side-gate to the great door of death. The souls of those who have died, beloved and unloved alike, walk in the great procession. The door of death is in reverse the door of birth. The souls of those who are on the way to be born are to be found there. Each person of us came through the door at birth and will return finally at death. Sleeping and waking are death and birth in miniature. Sleep takes the soul back into the world from where he was once born. Waking returns the soul to the person who lives and busies himself on earth. To carry the experiences of the universe in the conscious mind by day is too much for us. Overwhelmed, we forget, but not entirely. Out of the corner of the mind's eye, the great presences are caught as they pass. There are those who carry away some memory of these glimpses. But all is not goodness and light in the lands beyond sleep. Real beings of evil are there as much as those who serve and follow the good. For in part, all that is seen here has its origin there.

At each waking the mind comes back to the question: for what am I here today, why have I come through the door again? With the question comes the further thought: what could I do otherwise, and where is my place within the great procession in the heavens? There is no other room for actions of mine but here on earth. When I awaken and return to the body, I am a person in my own right, with a will of my own. Again and again the question returns: what for? what is the purpose of my own will? As many people as there are, so are there answers. There is one answer that has come from the mind of Christ himself. When he walked on earth, he lived on both sides of the door at once. He spoke the thoughts from the heavens in the world of earth. He told parables from time to time, using the language of pictures. One of these is the parable of the talents in St Matthew's Gospel. It is part of one of the last great speeches of Christ before the events of Easter. It follows the story of the future, of the wise and foolish virgins. It is followed by the scene of the great judgment. In between such lofty themes, as if it rightly belonged in such a setting, Christ handled the question of what an individual makes of his life here in this world from day to day. He did so in the picture of the sums money called 'talents' in older times.

Matthew 25:14-30

'It is like a man going on a journey; he called together his servants and entrusted his property to them. To one he gave five talents, to another two, to another one, to each according to his ability. Then he left the country. And he who had received the five talents at once began to work with them and gained another five. So also he who had been given two gained another two. But he who had been given one, went and hid his master's silver by burying it in the earth. When a long time had gone by, the master of the servants returned and settled accounts with them. First the one who had been given five talents came forward, bringing five more. He said, "Lord, five talents you gave me; see, I have gained another five." Then the master said, "You have done well, you good and faithful servant; you have faithfully tended a little, now I will make you a steward over much. You shall have a share of the joy of your master."

'Then the one who had been given two talents came forward and said, "Lord, two talents you gave me; see, I have gained another two." Then the master said to him, "You have done well, you good and faithful servant; you have faithfully tended a little, now I will make you a steward over much. You shall have a share of the joy of your master."

'Then the one who had been given one talent also came forward and said, "Lord, I know that you are a hard and stern man; you reap where you did not sow, you gather in

*where you did not distribute. I was afraid, and so I buried
your money in the earth. See, here you have what is yours
back again." Then the master answered, "You bad and idle
servant! You claim to know that I reap where I did not sow
and that I gather in where I did not distribute? Should you
then not all the more have taken my money to the money-
changers, so that, on my return, I could receive my property
together with the interest on it? Take the talent from him and
give it to the one who has ten talents." To him who has shall
be given, and he shall have in abundance; from him who
has not, even what he has will be taken. Cast the worthless
servant out into the darkness of external existence where there
is only wailing and gnashing of teeth.'*

The parable tells of the great, overriding purpose in human
existence as if it were a financial undertaking run for profit by
an owner lending out sums of money to borrowers. They are
expected to return the capital with increase at a later date. It is
about money making more money. Nevertheless the story has
hidden complications. The first question to ask about any parable
is what the various characters represent. Thereupon it transpires
that the capitalist in this story, with money to lend at a profit,
stands for the kingdom of heaven. Of him, it is said that he has
gone away into a far country but will one day return. There is
no rightful owner or master of this world but God himself and
he is absent. He has gone beyond the door that separates the
earth from the universe. That is to say, from the human angle,
the presence of God is to be found on the other side of sleep
and death. But he is nonetheless the owner. He initiates what is
undertaken here and determines the purpose for the future.

No parable was ever told in which a human being had the part
of an owner. This one is true to style. The human souls are the
servants, who are required to work within the undertaking of the
master, but are not controlled and supervised. Each one is made
responsible on his own account for a portion of the owner's

wealth and told to increase it. The servants are not said to have asked for this responsibility. The owner chose the course of action himself, when he left for another country.

What, according to the story, happened to the human servants? Each was given a number of coins or talents to handle according to the master's estimate of his ability. One received five, another two, and still another received one. But all had the same task – to trade with profit – each according to his own bent, and on his own responsibility. Each knew that he must set to work because he was one part in a great enterprise. The servant with five talents had ten ready for his master, and he with two, had four. Both doubled their outlay. He who received one did not rise to the challenge and merely buried the talent in the ground. He made no effort and took no risk. He was against the undertaking from the start.

The climax of the story is the return of the master after 'a long time'. He came back, as all the servants knew he would do one day. They were prepared although perhaps they did not know the exact moment. They all knew what he would expect. This parable is not about preparation as some others are, but about results. The master came to collect the profits. On the day of reckoning the servant with five talents and the one with two were, to his great content, able to give back the double of what they had received. At that moment the difference between them, which had been made at the outset in the master's estimate of their abilities, was wiped out thoroughly. Both received the same praise and the same promise. Although the master seemed intent upon profit throughout, he was not in fact a profiteer. He did not ask for the highest possible return for his money. He was satisfied, as the servants were, with double the outlay. Nor, strange in a financial enterprise, did he propose to share the profits with those who had produced them, nor to give them any obvious reward. Instead, he gave praise to each 'good and faithful servant'. Afterwards he promised a greater and harder responsibility for the future. He did not offer a holiday, leisure or security, but promotion, that is to say, more work and more risk. The new offer was made in a style that speaks for itself. There was in his mode of address a big change in the first words of praise to the next words of promise. At first he spoke to each one as 'servant' but then he said: 'I will make you steward over much.' The good servant was to become a master in his own right. Or, in modern terms, the reliable employees were to be taken into partnership. They were to share the joy of the master, which they could do if they were heart and soul in the enterprise. They could as servants rejoice in his praise, but as partners they could share his rejoicing that the business was flourishing as it should.

The servant who had buried his talent did not show himself stupid, when it was his turn to face the master. He had his line of defence well worked out and ready. He started by putting the blame on the master, instead of taking it himself, getting his accusation in first. You – he tried to say – are the hard one, imposing work and risk on others, while collecting the profit yourself. I was afraid of accepting conditions of that kind. I have not kept anything that belongs to you. Here you have safely back what you gave me and I am through with it. But although he was clever enough to accuse before he was accused, he did not escape the master's wrath. In no uncertain terms the master declared that the talents were intended to be used, not to be saved up even in safety. If the servant had not wanted to work with the money himself, he should have at least invested it with money lenders, who would pay interest. The other servants had increased the capital, but the last one, if he could not do that, should have seen that interest accrued to his talent. The master's anger was directed against allowing the money to lie idle. His reproach was on the same lines as his promise to the others. He insisted not on having permanent assets but on keeping the money moving to increase the scope and purpose of the whole enterprise.

The order was given to take the talent from the servant who had buried it uselessly and to give it to the one who already had most. This was not because he had money, but because he had shown that he knew how to use it and was prepared to continue doing so. 'To him who has shall be given ... from him who has not, even what he has shall be taken.' What a hard saying this would be in any other context! But since the good servants had already made their reckoning it was plain that they were not intended to accumulate wealth for themselves. They were to be partners and work harder than ever. It was only common sense to take the money away from the one who was not prepared to do anything with it and to give it to the one whose ability and energy were greatest. The worthless servant was thrown out of the business altogether, sacked out of hand; in reality he had thrown himself out at the time when he had purposely buried the talent.

This was not necessarily the end of his story. He had of course already missed the point of the master's enterprise. But the parables in the Gospels do not usually have a definite ending, and this one is no exception. 'Cast him into outer darkness; there shall be wailing and gnashing of teeth.' This is said of the worthless servant and it is to be found in other parables in identical words. The outer darkness is the place where the pain of exclusion can rouse the soul who was previously not awake to the situation. Pain is not in this sense punishment, but the stab of waking consciousness, the warning that something is wrong. The pain suffered by the excluded servant might be the beginning of new awareness, even perhaps of a future resolve to meet another opportunity in a better way. Whether the outer darkness would prove to be an end or a beginning has been left open, for only the excluded servant could decide himself.

How is the parable to be understood? Is the evolution of humankind on earth in reality a piece of big business for God? So the picture would seem to say, but it is not in fact constructed throughout in terms of business in the usual sense. The progress of the employees through their own energy and will towards higher responsibility is stressed more than the amount of profit they make. But a return for what is invested is called for nevertheless. When the evolution of the earth and of man is considered in the widest sense, it is clear that cosmic forces from the universe have been invested in the undertaking on a scale beyond imagination. We human beings cannot claim to have put ourselves together in body and soul nor to have constructed the world around us. We have use of what we have not made. We occupy a world we did not create. Have not the creating powers of the universe who serve the will of God a natural desire to see some return for what they have invested? They have offered a portion of themselves, the substance of their very being. Is it not the most natural thing to imagine that the human beings thus created are required to work with what has been lent to them, to make some contribution of their own? This is especially so since they are left to their own initiative, free from interference. But where are the talents? What do the sums of money represent?

Although the word 'talent' in the Gospel denoted a (considerable) weight of silver at the time, from this parable the other sense of the English word has grown. It can mean the inner riches of mind and body, by which we can be capable people. The world around likewise has its riches, which we learn to handle. Money is nothing in itself; its value is in what it represents. Here it stands for all the outer and inner resources with which human beings can work. It is increased when something is created by human effort, which is not provided by nature. All that is produced on earth by people themselves from inner resources is pictured in the talents which the servants earn over and above what has been loaned to them.

Humankind occupied a world created from the highest and most intricate wisdom. But love is not provided and must be created by human hearts. The warm, good, truth-filled substance of love is the return for which the divine investor looks at his coming. The worthless servant in the story said that he hid the talents because he was afraid. The good and faithful servants had courage. They began to create as much love as they had received wisdom and energy. But love is a mystery far beyond the usual meaning given to the word nowadays. Even in the parable itself it is not spoken of by word. A symbol is used instead, that of the sums of money, which the servants offered to the master over and above what they had received. If we remember that Christ himself thought out and told the story, it is clear that the substance of love for which no words were found is in the telling, since it is created out of the being of the storyteller himself.

To what time does the parable belong? When does the heavenly master appear for the reckoning? This event happens every time that the door is opened between the earthly and the heavenly worlds. The master is absent when the door is shut. It opens and he is here. His very presence has the effect of a judgment. The individual soul faces the reckoning on three levels. In one sense it comes with every falling asleep. The soul passes out of the body on the stream of will, which contains the unfinished, still emerging destiny. The soul comes into the body again at waking on the stream of past destiny, which is still in the process of being fulfilled. To experience the obligations coming over from the past and those accumulating for the future is to face a reckoning with one's self under the eyes of God. The mystery of human destiny made, suffered, and to be overcome, is the theme of sleeping and waking.

We sleep into our future and awaken to our past. On the next level of time we meet the larger reckoning at death and birth. We die into the future and are born out of the past. Dying, we gather up the patterns that we ourselves have woven into our lives. What shines brightly, what is inadequate, what is wrong, the well-begun design, the unfinished pieces, we take them all through the door to be sorted out by the powers gifted with higher wisdom than ours. We shall then find out what we have made of the loan with which we began and what must be done in the future. Being born, we start with these patterns that have been transformed from the destiny made in the past. With them we begin again, having a new loan from the powers of the universe, with which to enter once more the great enterprise of human history on earth.

At the highest level of time, the greatest reckoning of all will come, at the close of earth's evolution, at the end of the world. It is not for nothing that Chapter 25 of Matthew's Gospel ends with the picture of the judgment. The undertaking itself will be wound up and it will be known finally what has become of the loans made again and again. Will the owner have become wealthy through his investments? Nowhere in the parable is it said that he desired wealth for the sake of power or for the sake of retiring from a career in business. Only once is something said about his part in the undertaking. It is in the words of praise and promise spoken to each good and faithful servant, 'You shall have a share in the joy of your master.' In the original the word means joy in the sense of delight. The servant is to share in the delight of the master. What will he find in it to reward him? What can it be but delight in fresh, ever-continuing creation? How could the joy of the master mean lasting rest in doing nothing? Where is the finest delight but in creative action, in the energy to go on doing more and greater things?

The owner requires returns from the loans in order to start fresh undertakings. He promotes the servants to partners that they may continue to work with him in worlds to come beyond earthly time. The world in which we live now was created out of wisdom. That which is to come will be created out of love, the product of man's evolution here on earth. To be human is to be involved in the production of the substance for future creations. Such work can only be done on earth. We are engaged in it every day of our lives. The greatest reckoning is far off in the time to come, but it is linked with the passing hours of the day, the week and the year. 'When a long time had gone by, the master of the servants returned and settled accounts with them.'

A Parable of History

When Christ came to earth he found enemies. There were those who did not understand him, who were suspicious and afraid. But there were those who came to know well who he was, and yet were against him. It was they who planned and organised his death.

When Jesus was born in Bethlehem, according to the Evangelist Matthew, Herod tried to kill the child. He had the innocent children of Bethlehem massacred. They have since been honoured as the first martyrs for Christ's sake. Herod was the ruler in Galilee and Judea because he had the support of the Roman Emperor. So jealous was he of his position that he murdered some of his own descendants in fits of madness. Mad jealousy inspired him to attack the child whom he believed to be the Messiah.

Herod Antipas (a son of King Herod) caused John the Baptist to be beheaded. He did not know what he was doing; he did it against his better judgment. But a woman stood behind him, Herodias, who had knowledge and was possessed by hate. As the blow which was aimed at Jesus fell on the Innocents, so that aimed at Christ soon after his work began fell upon John.

The third attack was made upon Jesus Christ himself and no one could take it in his stead. The inner circle of Jewish priests, led by the High Priest who knew well what he did, brought about the condemnation and the death on Golgotha. The enemies who held him to be the Messiah wished and intended to kill. For what and why? It is clear that they were possessed by forces beyond human ones. There was nonetheless a human starting-point, jealousy turning to hate.

Surely, one might think, jealousy was in his case so out of place as to be impossible. How should this be? Did the human form of Jesus so conceal the divine being of Christ that the enemies did not grasp with whom they had to deal? It was not, at that period in history, difficult as it is today to believe in gods that really existed, nor was it considered impossible for the gods to take part in human affairs. The Jews honoured their famous prophets as divine messengers through whom Yahweh spoke directly. To be so overshadowed by a god that divine instructions could be delivered was known and accepted by tradition. Such 'supermen', possessed by more than human power and wisdom, were expected. They could be envied, because they were lifted beyond human limitations by the power working through them.

It is likely that the long-awaited Messiah was expected to appear in the manner of the old prophets. John the Baptist, it is clear, would have been welcome to the leaders of his people, who were unwilling to accept Jesus of Nazareth as the One for whom they waited. But John the Baptist refused the messiahship very definitely when the messengers of the priests followed him into the desert. At the beginning of St John's Gospel the scene is described in which he proclaimed three times his powerful 'no' to their questions. He was sent to be the messenger preparing the way, not to be himself the Messiah. Nothing that the highest authorities among his people could say could change his 'no' to 'yes'.

Jesus of Nazareth did not follow the expected pattern as did John in his appearance and behaviour. Even the place where he was brought up was pleasing only to some. Nazareth was a settlement under the care of the Essenes, a relgious order who had renounced the world of their time to prepare for the coming of the Messiah. They dwelt together in communities devoted to prayer and study. The leaders of the Jews, especially the priests, were in conflict with the Essenes, although they all lived for the coming of the Messiah. They resented the unworldliness of the members of the order, who on their part believed themselves to be the true guardians of the Jewish religion in contrast to the official priests with their worldly ambitions.

That Jesus came from Nazareth gave confidence to some of those around him that he was not a self-seeker, but it irritated others. On neither side of opinion could there be real satisfaction with the appearance which he presented as the Messiah. Jesus was too plain and simple for the Sadducees, those of the priestly families, who conducted affairs in the Temple at Jerusalem. He was too wise and straightforward in his teaching for the Pharisees, who admired intellectual brilliance. For the Essenes and others of the extreme persuasion, he was too much part of the world. They admired a way of life so ascetic that it made the ordinary things of existence of no account. Jesus in fact pleased no one of the self-appointed preparers for the Messiah, who wished a Messiah to appear who could not be overlooked or doubted. Probably not one of them had ever envisaged that there could be any doubt or uncertainty about who the Messiah was when he came. Unmistakable signs were expected, plain even to the unbeliever. The last thing that anyone imagined was the appearance of someone about whom each person had to make up his mind for himself, and who would ask, 'Who do you say that I am?'

It was all the more difficult for those around to grasp who Jesus Christ actually was after his mission began, because until he was thirty years old he was not in truth the Messiah, although he was so to become. He was a very highly prepared person, with a heredity selected through long generations and with a personality distinguished by the purest devotion and wisdom. Undoubtedly to those who met him in the early years he must have been the pattern of a good man, the ideal of what goodness could humanly be. Nevertheless, he was not the Messiah until, in the hour when he was baptised in the River Jordan by John, the Spirit of Christ descended to inhabit his soul and his body. Christ in Jesus, the Son of God in man, was the Messiah. His first act at his coming was to withdraw into the wilderness. When he began to work, moving with a band of followers from place to place, teaching and healing, he took up the pattern known by many examples at the time. He did nothing out of fashion from the outer aspect. Those with eyes to see and ears to hear knew that in meeting him they met more than just another itinerant preacher, one among many. But only towards the end of his life on earth did he become a recognised public figure.

Some perplexed people asked him for a sign but he offered them in answer just two pictures from the old mysteries that had been known for many generations. He spoke of the Queen of Sheba who came to visit Solomon and of the prophet who descended into the great fish. Neither of these could constitute a sign in the meaning of the request. They refer to nothing external but, instead, to the inner quality of faith. The queen was filled with the innocent quality of wonder. She came to Solomon because she saw that his wisdom was greater than hers: she came and she saw. In the same sense, Jesus Christ said to those round him: 'Come and see.' The prophet resisted the divine message that he should go to Nineveh. But then realised that by submitting his own will he would find it again on a higher level: he listened and obeyed. He had to descend into the darkness and came forth from his ordeal renewed. Such were the examples put forward by Jesus Christ.

The open mind in thinking and the willingness to be born again are the means of beholding Christ. When he walked on earth in the body of Jesus, he could be recognised by the eye of faith, but he was never recognised by external means, either then or now. His presence was a secret, for no one knew without seeing with the eye of faith. Such a situation was quite unexpected to most of those who earnestly awaited the Messiah and they were sadly at a loss.

Had the Messiah appeared with unmistakable signs of power,

he would have been raised beyond the reach of human jealousy. Why this did not happen was put into words by himself at the trial before Pilate. 'My kingdom is not of this world.' He did not come, as Herod feared, to take the place of any king or ruler. He came to lead the way to the kingdom of heaven. The jealousies that he encountered were in fact quite beside the point. He never provoked or gave cause for the fears of his enemies. They were self-induced through ambitions that had nothing to do with the coming of the true Messiah, who would not compete for the glories of this world. The jealousy was nonetheless real and strong. It was effective in that it brought about the Crucifixion.

The jealousy of Herod caused him to have murdered the little children of Bethlehem, at the time when Jesus was born. A similar jealousy was felt by his descendant, who persecuted John the Baptist. These kings reigned in the Holy Land without a real title to the throne, put there by the authority of the Emperor in Rome. It left the Herods in the uneasy position of behaving as if they were the chosen kings of their people, when they ruled in fact by force. The genuine Jews knew the line of descent from King David exactly. It was the same as that described by St Matthew when he listed the generations of the forefathers of Jesus. When the crowds later on would hail Jesus as 'Son of David' they were calling for their true king, for their spiritual leader, but at the same time for one of the true earthly descent.

The jealousy of the Herods was for their own power and glory. Another jealousy on a much grander scale emanated from Rome itself. Later the early Christians were to feel the brunt of it for long periods. It was never satiated, for the Death on the Cross of Jesus Christ did not appease it. The jealousy of the Herods was human, but the Roman kind was that of a god for a god. It was of superhuman proportions and lasted as long as the urge inspiring the emperors of Rome continued. During the period in which the Roman republic turned into an empire, there was a widespread fever of expectation for the One who was to come. The Jews felt the expectation to be peculiarly their own, but in all other religions the coming was foretold. A god of the highest order was awaited who would solve the dilemma of human existence.

It was a natural development of the Roman outlook that when emperors arose – men with vast power in this world – that the human and divine became confused. The Greeks had had many tales which the Romans took as their own of gods visiting the earth in hours of decision to intervene in human destiny. In the minds of most people living at that time such events were wonderful but quite credible. Who, at that time, could better seem to be the fulfilment of this expectation but the Emperor in Rome, dominating not just his own people but the nations of the civilized world? He was the most important person present, with most to give to those who asked for boons and the greatest power to make or mar. He was, in the popular outlook of the age, the one whom it was easy and beneficial to hail as the promised god. The Emperor Augustus first, and his descendants later, were given the title 'Divine' while they lived and ruled. They became living gods by human consent. Another living god, a Messiah in Jerusalem, could only seem to be a rival to the divine ruler in Rome. God for god, city for city, power for power, how could there be a more dreadful jealousy than this?

The priests and rulers of the Jews felt jealousy of still another kind. They identified themselves with their nation and their nation with their religion. At the heart of their religion was the expectation of the Messiah. It was for them to receive the coming god, for he was to be of their nation. All other peoples of the world would look towards Jerusalem to find the Saviour. His guardians would be the priests of the Jewish Temple. He would be approached, petitioned and prayed to through them. Their influence in the affairs of men would be more subtle and all-pervading than that of the Emperor with his army. Their Messiah would be both the High Priest and the God himself. The priests of the Jews may well have expected Jerusalem to become the shrine of the Messiah, the holiest in the whole wide world, and themselves his all-powerful priests. Their religion would dominate all others, their Temple outshine the rest, their priest-king be the living God in person by divine right. In Rome a king aspired to become a god by human consent, but in Jerusalem the Messiah would reign on earth by the will of God himself. How could they be prepared to accept a Messiah who said: 'My kingdom is not of this world?' It is unlikely that they were in doubt that Jesus Christ was in truth the Messiah, but the style of his appearance would be useless to their way of thinking.

The jealousy that has lastly to be taken into account is that of Judas. One of the Twelve, accepted into the closest companionship with Jesus Christ, hearing, seeing and experiencing all that happened, how could he become the betrayer? How could he, who should have been able to have given the kiss of friendship, become able to give the false one? In St John's Gospel it is said plainly that during the Last Supper Satan entered into him. He became possessed by the Evil One, whose whole urge was to destroy. The human enemies of Christ would not have actually believed that by killing him they could destroy more than the body. To kill someone by their standards was to put him out of the way, to send him back to the divine world, so that he would cease to disturb this one. But Satan, being himself divine though Evil, could be expected to intend something more. He held the power of death itself in his devil's hands. Since death belongs to this world and could be encountered by Christ only by coming to earth, a struggle of cosmic powers was to be faced. Christ and Satan were aware of what was involved. It was beyond the scope of Judas. He became an instrument manipulated by Satan.

Although Judas was not completely responsible, the question still remains of how he could allow himself to come so far under the satanic influence. How did he let Satan in? Jealousy was the means. He had expected the Messiah to be a god and to reign as one on earth. He had not expected the modest leader, who walked his ways on earth, restraining his divine authority, refusing kingship. Beyond this point it is only possible

141

to conjecture what Judas felt. Maybe he resented the human character of Jesus. A man meant little at that period. Many a one was bought and sold into slavery. Judas sold Jesus himself and for a poor price. Maybe he wanted the god and not the man, and was jealous that a divinity could take human form and suffer such reduced circumstances. His was the jealousy of the human for the more than human, for the One having power that he would not use. He may, like the two disciples who argued the point at the Last Supper, have hoped to be raised to a more than human eminence because of his nearness to the Messiah. So often when he wished Christ to declare himself, he must have only seen Jesus. Was he jealous of Jesus for the sake of Christ? Perhaps our imagination can only touch the edge of such a mystery as that of the betrayal.

Matthew 21:28–46

'What do you think? A man had two sons. He went to the first and said, "Son, go and work in the vineyard today." He answered, "Yes, sir." But he did not go. Then he went to the second and said the same to him. He answered, "I will not." Later, however, he regretted his answer and went after all. Which of the two did the will of the father?' They said, 'The second.' Jesus said, 'Yes, I say to you, the tax-collectors and the harlots will find access to the kingdom of God more readily than you. John came to you in the way of God's order and harmony, but you would not listen to him. Yet the tax-collectors and the harlots opened their hearts to him. You saw it, and even then you did not change your hearts and minds and respond to him.

'Hear another parable: There was a man, the master of a house. He planted a vineyard and surrounded it with a fence and dug a winepress in it and built a tower. Then he handed it over to the vine-growers and went away to another country. When the grape-season came, he sent his servants

to the vine-growers to receive his fruit. But the vine-growers
took hold of the servants; they beat one, killed another and
stoned the third. Then he sent out servants anew, a greater
number than the first time. But they treated them in the
same way. Lastly he sent his son to them, because he said
to himself: My son they will respect. But when the vine-
growers saw the son, they said to themselves: This is the heir.
Come, let us kill him, then we will have his inheritance.
And they took him and threw him out of the vineyard and
killed him. Now when the lord of the vineyard comes, what
will he do to those vine-growers?' They said, 'He will repay
evil with evil and destroy them. And the vineyard he will
give to other vine-growers, who will deliver to him the fruits
of the vineyard at harvest time.' And Jesus said to them,
'Have you never read this passage in the scriptures:

"The stone which the builders regarded as useless has
become the corner stone. The Lord himself so shaped it, and
our eyes see it with wonder?"

'Therefore I tell you: The kingdom of God will be taken
away from you and be given to a people who allow the fruits
of the kingdom to ripen. And whoever runs against this stone
will be dashed to pieces; and he on whom it falls will be
crushed.'

When the chief priests and the Pharisees heard his
parables, they knew that he was speaking about them. And
they tried to get him into their power, but they were afraid of
the people, for all held him to be a prophet.

In St Matthew's Gospel there is a parable addressed to the
enemies so plainly put that it roused their fear. When the chief
priests and Pharisees heard the parable they perceived that he
was speaking about them. It tells of a landowner, who planted
a vineyard and equipped it with a hedge or a fence, a winepress
and a tower. He then let it to tenants and departed abroad. But
it was still his and at harvest time he sent for the produce. Twice

he sent servants, who not only did not receive what was due but were also badly treated and even killed. On the third occasion the owner sent his son. But he too was cast out of the vineyard and was slain. The parable ends with a question to the audience of enemies: 'When the lord of the vineyard comes, what will he do to those vine-growers?' They reply that he will take his revenge.

Christ does not speak of vengeance himself. He simply asked the audience to complete the story. They did so, speaking for themselves and, as it turned out, about themselves. Had these priests and Pharisees in reality accepted Jesus Christ as the Messiah? Is that why they were so filled with fear and anger? They accepted at once the picture of the bad tenants as applied to themselves, thereby acknowledging Christ as the son who was slain and God as the owner. They did not deny the picture. God at the beginning made this world and then withdrew leaving it to be inhabited and cultivated by people. They were left to themselves but nevertheless they owed him the produce. That this is a true picture of earth-evolution was never in dispute. But what have the human tenants done in God's vineyard? They have worked so hard that it has borne fruit. But they became so greedy for possession that they forgot that it was on loan. Having worked, they became anxious to be owners and became in fact thieves. Being thieves at heart, they became murderers likewise. This stemmed from the original strong desire to possess the vineyard for themselves. They set out to dismiss the owner, the servants and the son. The priests and Pharisees, with many others of the same mind who have come after them, have intended to take over from God.

The ultimate jealousy is the original one, man's jealousy of God. Genesis tells of the first jealousy to have been deliberately roused in Adam and Eve by the serpent, Lucifer. Pointing to the forbidden apple on the tree in Paradise, he said, 'Your eyes will be opened, and you will be like God, knowing good and evil.' And Eve listened. 'So when the woman saw that the tree ... was to be desired to make one wise, she took of its fruit and ate'

(Gen.3:5f). So by theft the first man and woman were said to have taken for themselves the knowledge of good and evil, which belonged to God. They were possessed by Lucifer's jealousy; later, Judas, a disciple called to follow Christ, became possessed by the jealousy of Satan.

Adam and Eve lost their original existence within the divine presence and found themselves in a hard world of their own. 'Cursed is the ground because of you,' said God to Adam, 'in toil you shall eat of it all the days of your life ... In the sweat of your face you shall eat bread till you return to the ground, for out of it you were taken' (Gen.3:17–19). The presence of God was withdrawn. The earth became the vineyard of the parable, still under divine ownership, but inhabited and worked in by man. But the jealousy persisted. Once, man had been made jealous of God's knowledge. Then he became jealous of his power in the earth, of his right to the fruits produced in the course of evolution. Jealousy of wisdom became jealousy of power. When Christ came to reconcile the world of earth to the divine world, one jealousy arose from another. God had once dismissed man from Paradise, then man, or rather one portion of humankind, wanted to dismiss the Son of God from the earth.

What did the tenants, in terms of the parable, intend to do with the vineyard when they took possession? The owner was waiting for the produce with the aim of using it, not in the vineyard but in the spheres of existence into which he had withdrawn. He required what had been produced on earth for the sake of the heavens. The tenants wanted to keep the harvest for themselves, to use on earth what had been produced there. Within the logic of the story, they wanted the wine for themselves. In the sphere of plant-life, the juice of the grape corresponds to the blood as it flows in the human body. Both are portions of the mystery of evolving selfhood, that spiritual power which human beings have not brought with them but which grows and develops here on earth. It is that through which human souls become capable of love. In all the life of the earth wisdom is found to be at work. It

145

is only from within the being of humans, when they no longer live under the divine protection but go through trial and error on their own, that love evolves in freedom. As the wine is made from the juice of the grape, so from the blood in which the force of the self, or ego, dwells the capacity to create love is distilled. It is in the nature of love that it does not remain with the one who produces it. The love grown on earth within human beings flows rightly out to the spirit of God, who receives it into his divine existence. Love creates and will create in the universe of God.

When instead of true selfhood its false opposite is at work, the self grasps and holds that which it should offer beyond itself. The force that should flow out in creative love hardens into egotism. There exists that dark power of egotism which aims to hold on to the existence of the earth as it is now and prolong it beyond the time when it should rightly end. Christ has become the guardian of earth-evolution and will lead it towards the right ending in world-death. To die is to pass from the earthly to the spiritual. This world must finally spiritualise in death. But the powers of evil have other aims. They inspire the wish to prolong the present, material state of existence, to give it an artificial immortality. This world would then be frozen into a condition that would be living death, induced by the ultimate egotism, the will that refuses to make the offering, that keeps what it should give. In terms of world-evolution, the tenants of the story, who slew the owner's son in order to take possession of the earth's vineyard, are those who join in the jealous intentions for the earth's future of the powers of evil.

This parable is distinctive among the others for its connection with what was happening in history at the time. It mirrors the aims of those who were preparing to attack and slay Jesus Christ. They recognised the truth of the story, but far from treating it as a warning they hastened to confirm it by their actions. In their haste they did not wait to hear how the story might have continued or changed if Christ, instead of themselves, had given it an ending. It remains as they ended it, a story of judgment and condemnation, the history of what the original Fall into evil had made of man. Imprisoned in jealousy, many people could only continue in the Fall, even when Christ offered the opportunity to rise again. Outside the parables, in the sphere of historical happening, Judas repeated the story. He awoke to what he had done, threw back to the priests the price of betrayal, and hanged himself in the hour of the Crucifixion. He saw as far as death and no further. Christ himself went further. Accepting the death on the Cross, he overcame it and rose to new life. He was not dismissed from the earth but triumphed over death, taking upon himself in the spirit the care of human evolution to the end. The tenants wished to eject the son from the vineyard by slaying him. But at the Resurrection he nevertheless made it into his own, that he might in the fullness of time offer it, with the harvest, back to the father to whom it is rightly due.

The Prodigal Son

Has history a meaning? If so, what kind of meaning? From time to time thinkers have agreed with the old prophet that there is nothing new under the sun. So much that seems new has been there before, even to the first model of a modern Communist state found in China in the eighth century. Other thinkers see history as a line of continuous discovery and progress from the primitive to the modern. It is doubtful whether the human behaviour of today bears inspection from this point of view. Still other thinkers compose chains of cause and effect, watching one thing lead to another with inexorable force. Others see blind urges in operation working with a will that comes either by itself from no one knows where, or, if the mind revolts at that, from the hidden intentions of God.

Can it be said that anywhere in the Gospels the question of the purpose in history is considered and handled? If they are rightly read, the parables will be found to contain a far-reaching philosophy of history set forth not in intellectual concepts but in the pictures of imaginative thinking. The philosopher who unfolds its meaning is Christ himself. The ideas come direct from the world of God, to which he belongs. Belief in God can be a vague tenet of the mind. Or it can become an inner sense of the soul that responds to the wonder of all that lives and unfolds around and within oneself. There is a sense for what is divine, as there is for beauty, for art or for music. The philosophy of the parables will not be understood without it. How could it be otherwise, when they are the stories composed and told by Christ himself, in whom the divine presence lived on earth?

Today we are accustomed to many pictures of world-evolution, in which the sense for the divine has been omitted on the excuse that the pictures of evolution are scientific. The question is, can such pictures be taken from reality, when this sense of the mind is left out? They could be scientific and quite unreal. Rudolf Steiner saw this danger coming and put forward a new idea of science, in which the sense for the divine is allowed a real function in knowledge. He put God and man into the picture of world-evolution. If man is omitted, there is no purpose, and if God is omitted, there is no higher wisdom and informed will. Such an idea of history meets the philosophy of the parables on its own ground.

Luke 15:11–32

And he went on: 'There was a man who had two sons, and the younger of them said to his father, "Father, give me the share of the property that falls to me." So he divided his estate between them. A few days later the younger son took the whole of his share and left home for a distant country, where he wasted his substance in reckless living. And when he had spent everything, a severe famine arose in that country and he began to be in need. So he went and joined himself to one of the citizens of that country who sent him on to his farm to feed the pigs. He would gladly have fed on the husks that the pigs were eating, but no one gave him anything.

'Then he came to himself and said: How many of my father's hired servants have more food than they can eat and here am I, starving to death! I will arise and go to my father and I will say to him, "Father, I have sinned against heaven and before you. I am no longer worthy to be called your son, treat me as one of your hired servants." And he arose and came to his father. But while he was still a long way off, his father saw him and had compassion on him. He ran to meet

*him, embraced him and kissed him. And the son said to
him, "Father, I have sinned against heaven and before you.
I am no longer worthy to be called your son." But the father
said to his servants, "Quick, fetch a robe, my best one, and
put it on him, and put a ring on his hand and shoes on his
feet. Bring the fatted calf and kill it, and let us have a feast
to celebrate the day, for this my son was dead and is alive
again, he was lost and is found."*

*'And they began to make merry. Now his elder son was
in the field; and as he came and drew near to the house, he
heard music and dancing. And he called one of the servants
and asked what this meant. And he said to him, "Your
brother has come, and your father has killed the fatted calf
for joy that he has received him safe and sound." But he
was angry and would not go in. His father came out and
invited him, but he said to his father, "Look, I have served
you for many years, and I have never disobeyed one of your
commandments; yet you never gave me a kid so that I might
make merry with my friends." But when this son of yours
comes, who has wasted your property with harlots, for him
you kill the fatted calf! But he said to him, "My child, you
are always with me, and all that is mine is yours. You
should rejoice and be glad, for this your brother was dead and
is alive; he was lost and is found".'*

Christ's account of history is found in all the parables, but in
its most concentrated form in one especially – the story of the
Prodigal Son. It is the centre and hub of the whole pattern of
parables found in the Gospels of Matthew, Mark and Luke.
Nevertheless it is told only by St Luke in the fifteenth chapter.
The inner meaning of world-history is its theme. It starts right at
the beginning of time with the Father.

There is a style common to all the parables. They speak in
pictures well known to human experience, but what happens
within them is something quite different from the ordinary. The

parable of the Prodigal Son begins with the father, a householder and owner of property, who has two sons. The elder stays at home helping to manage the estate. The younger asks to leave home, taking his rightful share of the inheritance with him. That, as far as it goes, could happen anywhere and at any time. But it turns out that there are strange features in the story. When the younger son leaves home, he goes to a country far away, where conditions are quite different from those he has known. He leaves behind the good order and conduct of his father's house. All at once he can do what pleases him without restraint, because in the new country there is no reaction from the world around to his sayings and doings. But he is utterly ignorant of how to go on under the new conditions.

The question arises: was the father as ignorant as the son about life in the strange land? Was he unable to advise, warn or prepare him for the adventure? How could he let him go, if he was himself ignorant? If he did know more, why did he send him, well provided with wealth, but quite unequipped with training or instruction? The picture is formed in the early part of the story of a great risk, taken knowingly or unknowingly, with an inexperienced young son. How could a good, wise father behave so? But this is no ordinary earthly father. He is the chief character in the divine drama in which the purposes of history are unfolded. Only the bearing of God himself could take a risk of such proportions, on such a scale.

When the younger son arrives in the far country, he finds others there before him. The parables are written in a very sparse style, leaving much to be read between the lines. What will be read depends upon the character of the story itself. If it is understood that in this parable the father of the sons represents God, then the far country where his rule does not prevail can only be the world of earth in contrast to the Father's house in the heavens. A long process of cosmic evolution has been necessary to bring about on earth the conditions which we know here and take for granted. In the beginning heaven and earth were one within the divine order. The presence of God prevailed throughout. Then the process of separation began. Two worlds came about, divided by the great cosmic void. The earth continued to bear the image of the original creation by God but ceased to be sheltered within his existence. It became the place where other purposes than his could be unfolded, where the restraint of his will and order was removed. It became God-forsaken, the place where anything could happen. The first beings to find an outlet for their impulses under such conditions were the princes of evil who work against the will of God. In the heavens their activity is restrained. On earth they can have free play with their efforts.

There is not one devil but two, divided in their aims, which are indeed opposite, but united in their opposition to the will of the Father. Each has the ambition to make a kingdom for himself in the image of his own intentions. Lucifer yearns to build an upper world in the clouds, peopled with sham angels, good and nice but without will or responsibility. Ahriman wants to fashion an underworld, where matter is the final reality and mechanics prevail. A living machine, inhabited by real beings, who have become cogs within it, run by his own master mind, is his hope and aim. When the younger son arrives in the far country of earth, the arch-devils are there before him, preparing their purposes. Of course they would both wish to get hold of the new arrival, all the better from their angle for being a greenhorn. What is a kingdom without inhabitants, a king without subjects? The two devils are rivals in aim but companions in their intention to seize for their own ends the young man and his wealth.

And he? How is he to know? He has never left the shelter of his father's house before, has never known the divine order disturbed, has never heard falsehood. Those who are not what they seem are outside his ken. The very intention to turn against the divine will and act independently has never entered his mind and is so foreign to him that he cannot grasp it. How should he deal with companions of the calibre of the two devils without falling into trouble? Who is this innocent but witless person with so much at his disposal that is not of his own making? It is man himself, he who in medieval parlance was known as Everyman. The younger son of the father, who has left home and gone to the world across the void from which the divine presence has been withdrawn, is man. It is the place where the devils have also found the opportunity of making their home. The father has accepted his urge to become independent, but he has not given to the son the knowledge of the land in which he will find himself. He has given him powers of mind and body to use at will. He has prepared the varied world in which he will use them. But he takes the biggest of all risks with him.

Everyman arrives with no real effort of his own in the far country and at once turns into a wastrel. He has always been provided for and he still has resources in plenty. But he does not know how to husband them nor to use them with purpose. The two devils and their followers have no wish to teach him. They are willing enough to help him exploit his advantages as long as they last. But Everyman is in for his first shock, for which experience has not prepared him. The wealth is dissipated and comes to an end. What the father has given him from his own store will not last when it is only enjoyed and not put to use. Everyman, who has never known concern for the morrow, stands bereft of all that he thought was his. He has consumed everything, undertaken nothing, and all is at an end.

Because this story is about human history and not ordinary affairs, another element enters in at this point. When Everyman has wasted his portion, a famine sets in. The earth itself goes to waste and cannot give the food which he needs. He has to go hungry. This is the second experience to which he has been a stranger until now. Why should the earth go to waste because Everyman is a wastrel? Looking around at what happens in our world today, it is easy to observe how the earth is being now laid to waste by the very human beings whose lives depend on its fertility. It is considered quite natural nowadays that its resources should be exploited to the point that the ground absorbs poisons that do not disappear, the air is polluted and the vitality, from which our own is nourished, is depleted. Our modern plagues and diseases are produced by scientific means. No generation has so much reason to understand this feature in the story, that Everyman, having wasted his substance, has also brought about the famine.

What is he to do? In face of his new experiences of loss and hunger, he wakes up and does something to help himself. He does not fall into self-pity nor show a sense of grievance. Perhaps he has begun to realise that he has brought the situation on himself. He goes out to get a job and takes one at the humblest level, being so unused to work that he could hardly expect anything better. He becomes a swineherd and is prepared in his need to eat with the pigs that he keeps. But they are only given husks, that is to say 'pig-waste'. It is one of the remarkable features of pigs that they have such a talent for digestion that they can transform left-overs their into rounded layers of fat. Other animals do marvels with digestion, but they demand better material to work on before they can provide human food.

The pigs of this story can exist even on the husks available in time of famine. But not so Everyman. The pigs are so much at one with their surroundings that, like all other animals, they can live entirely from what they receive from the earth. It is the nature of animals to have in this world only that part of themselves that can happily belong here. Their spiritual part never descends but remains aloof in the realm of the heavens – this is the source of their self-sufficiency. From the heavens they receive the surpassing wisdom of their instincts, from the earth their sustenance. But man is not so constituted. His spirit must descend to dwell wholly within his earthly part, but nevertheless remain a stranger in this world. He is never quite at ease, never completely adjusted to what is around him. He is always aware that his inner self really belongs elsewhere and can find his true home only in the worlds of spirit. He has needs that cannot be satisfied on earth. He is hungry for the food of the spirit. Because of this hunger, he is human and cannot live like the animals. So it comes about that Everyman cannot share the husks with the pigs. He must starve without the bread that is eaten in the house of the father.

'Then he came to himself ...' In the blank of despair something awakens within him, which he has never known before. His will had woken up when he took the job as swineherd. Now his thinking is roused. He recognises what has become of himself and what position is now his. It is a painful awakening, for he has to realise what it means that his wealth is lost and his opportunities wasted. At that moment he also recognises that he cannot live without the food that comes from the father's house. His spirit can only be fed by that which belongs to the divine spirit of the world. But what is he to do? How can he have the true bread except by returning to the father's house? He must return or perish. But he has not behaved like a true son. What then? He resolves to go back and offer himself as a servant. He has worked in the far country. He will offer to work for the father and to earn the bread that he needs so urgently. It is a big decision, for it means acknowledging his failure, giving up the pride of sonship and not asking to have back again what has been lost. It is not said whether he has reason to expect that the father would take pity on him or if he simply refuses to ask for help. He relies in fact on the plan which he has thought out for himself and on his own strength of will to put it into action.

How hard a road back, compared with the easy way by which he had set out! Sad and hungry, taking each step by an effort of will, facing the prospect of arriving home a failure, the son makes his way onwards. He starts out on an impulse of courage, prompted by desperate need. But his thoughts and feelings necessarily change as he struggles along. This is no journey that would leave someone the same at the end as he was at the start. It is a pilgrimage of soul leading towards the attainment of a higher kind of selfhood. What might be an egotistical touch in the motives of hunger and need at the beginning would be transformed into a purer and truer longing for the home of the spirit in the father's house. His awareness of the need of all his fellow men for the true bread of the soul would become stronger than the concern for his own salvation.

The question arises how the witless, helpless Everyman of the first part of the story became capable of the courage and striving of the one who went back alone in the second part. What can explain so great a transformation? There is nothing, if the outer events of the tale are considered. But, between the lines, the thread of an inner theme is intertwined with the outer one. When Christ told the parable, he did not, to outer appearance, bring himself into it. Yet he is there, so closely identified with Everyman that he speaks with his words and acts in his actions. When Everyman comes to himself, it is Christ who speaks in his heart. When he courageously takes the road back alone, it is Christ who works in his will. He goes with him every step of the way, not at his side, but hidden in the innermost parts of his being. He has come to the help of Everyman at the lowest point in the tragedy of loss and failure. He has not rescued him from his troubles. He has made his future into his own business, sharing with him the strength of his spirit. Filled with Christ-given courage, Everyman climbs to the end the road of salvation.

The father, full of compassion, runs to meet the son, as soon as he can be seen from the house. It cannot be that he has known nothing of his fate and his struggle. But, having risked the son's all in the far country, he must go through with it to the conclusion. He must wait and watch until Everyman finishes the journey back by himself. In the joy and enthusiasm of his welcome, the son cannot make the whole of his prepared speech. He goes so far as to confess his unworthiness to be still called the son, when he is interrupted. The father sends the servants for the gifts which will explain more clearly than words what kind of place he will now take in the household. He is clad in a new robe, the best in the store, which must have been long saved up for a more than ordinary occasion. All the members of the household can see that he is still the son of the house, but marked with a distinction which was not his before. He is treated like a guest from outside who brings honour to his hosts by his coming. A ring is put on his hand, a symbol of the authority born of an inner, well-tried integrity. He puts on new shoes. The feet, whose every step on the way back have been made out of deliberate courage, will carry him henceforth to new, significant actions.

He is established as a person raised to a new dignity in his own right by the apparel which the father gives him to wear. He is not restored to being the person he was before he suffered the tragedy in the far country. He is not now to be the child of his father, but the son who has left home and returns, bringing that with him which could only be found and won through the venture into another world. He is the one who 'was dead and is alive; he was lost and is found'.

The mystery of the Trinity lives in the scene of reunion in the father's house. The Father-god, who has taken the risk of sending his child out alone, receives the son, in whom lives and works the creating power of the Son-god, who has gone from heaven to earth in search of him. The longing for the spirit in the heart of the lost son has changed on the hard journey back into enlightenment. The Holy Spirit has begun to shine in his thinking and to work in his willing. At the homecoming of Everyman, Father, Son and Holy Spirit meet in the joy of a venture well accomplished, of a great purpose fulfilled. God becoming man has raised up Everyman out of death to be man become the Son of God.

What of the elder brother who comes late on the scene from his work in the fields, after the feast of welcome has already begun? Many other sons of God besides man live, move and have their being in the universe. The order of existence depends upon their wisdom and strength working in service to the will of God. They are part and parcel of his being, yet distinguished by their characters and their tasks. Taken together in community, they are known in Christian doctrine as the hierarchies, or 'the company of heaven'. They have never known the parting from the father, the venture into the far country, the temptations and the opportunities. But they are aware of the portion of wealth which Everyman took with him at his departure. And they know waste when they see it. The elder brother, who represents them in the parable, speaks for them when he complains to the father of the welcome given to the wastrel on his return. The elder brother is a good manager and a sturdy worker. The younger has been on his adventures and has brought nothing back to show for what he took with him. It is not hard to imagine that angels, archangels and all the company of heaven can be dissatisfied when they look from their angle into the affairs of human beings. They may well ask when we are going to give back some return for all that we have so plentifully received from them. Everyman must face the judgment of the elder brother, of every spirit of God who asks: what has become of that which we have given you to have and to use?

Did the elder brother finally join the feast? The parable provides no answer. Its last words are those of the father, explaining that this is the son, who was dead and is alive again, was lost and is found. Perhaps in the course of history it is not yet known whether or not he will accept the explanations. The father has a greater vision than his. He knows that the good order of the universe, faithfully maintained through the ages by the company of heaven, is not enough. The universe may not be allowed to run down, unprovided with the seed for a new creation in the future. The old order cannot produce it. A new impulse is necessary. It is to be born out of that which is found again out of loss, resurrected out of death. It will be produced only out of the inner being of man, when that which was given to him is lost and his own power of will has woken within him. The father says to the elder son: you have faithfully maintained all that continues from the past, but your lost brother brings home to the universe the seed for the future.

The father took a vital risk with the younger son because it was necessary for the future of evolution. The other brother of Everyman, Christ, gave the sacrifice of himself to bring the new impulse of creation into history. What is dead can become alive again. What was lost is found because he performed on Golgotha the cosmic deed that only the foremost of the Sons of God could accomplish. He chose the earth as the place and the body of a man as the instrument to do what he intended. He it is who through his deed of life and death gives meaning and purpose to our history on earth. Everyman may start back to the father's house in the first place for his own sake. When he arrives, he is the messenger of what is to come.

Postscript

All the books which we open in order to learn something are not bound volumes on the shelves of the library. The world around us is like a great open book, which we continually consult as we have our experiences, but which we can also refuse to read. 'Books in the running brooks, sermons in stones' (Shakespeare, *As You Like It*) are there for everyone and are found likewise in the mountains and the seas, in the fields and in the forests. The various affairs that people go about are included in the book, along with the doings of the animals that have long supplied us with fables. When we live in the pictures of the parables, we find that all these things are the alphabet of a language in which spiritual things can be expressed. The book of the world does not provide symbols or allegories, but realities with a spiritual origin. In their earthly appearance, they are separated from their true meaning but become transparent again when they are joined to it once more. When this happens, the language is discovered which is that of the parables.

These stories seem to have made a world of their own, complete with inhabitants and scenery. In reality it is the world that we know otherwise but illuminated with a different light. There are no weird people or fanciful creatures to be met with but just those doing sensible things, like sowing seed, tending vineyards, going on journeys or holding festivals. They are not even always hard at work but can be seen at their merrymaking. What they do is for sound purposes, like getting a good harvest, doubling an investment, arranging a son's marriage. These things are done under real conditions, where weeds grow among good seed, where small seeds become large plants, where fish of every kind are caught in a net. But however familiar the alphabet of this language may be, the meaning is not to be found in our experience here. What is said in the parables comes from the ideas in the mind of God himself.

It is necessary to consider each word and picture in these stories in its own original meaning. One should ask: what is the true nature of a king? What is the kingliness of a king? He will wear a crown. It will shine on his head, representing the aura of wisdom shining from his spirit. He will have a kingdom, a sphere of influence in which his will prevails, reinforced by his armies. He will have much to give because much is in his hands and giving is part of his office. Is a father spoken of? The picture of true fatherliness should be brought into the world. He is able to set free, but he continues to care deeply, to watch and to wait. He never ceases to give but he always discriminates. It is the same when a story tells of a shepherd, a merchant or a fisherman. It is necessary to imagine what each is doing in his kind of work in order to realise what spiritual activity it reflects here on earth. Those types of work that belong to the original pattern of human life are repeating on a small scale the activities of God in the universe. When the language of the parables is read in such a way, it begins to reveal its deeper meaning.

All this is so because the world in which we live here was brought forth by divine action. It reflects in earthly form that which exists and has its being in the heavens. The parables are composed on the principle that the world is God's place because it was created out of his thought and will, and man is made in his image. God, having produced the language of the world-book, used it to reveal himself to men and women through their experience of life on earth. Then Christ came into this world. He brought the new revelation, turning the pages of the book to write on them the continuation of what was already known.

He spoke of what God had done from the beginning and of what he himself had come to do in the future. Events were to be written into the book of this world that were not already present in the spheres of the heavens. Divine history was to be made among people on earth, who were to join by their own effort in the making. What God had begun in the heavens was to be fulfilled here. So it comes about that the parables are put into the language of the created world but that they speak of meanings and happenings never known before.

We hear of a shepherd watching over his sheep, but doing something more beyond his duty, of a housewife sweeping, but her task turns into a drama beyond the ordinary, of a father with two sons, but one does not follow the usual course. The drama is transformed from the well-known pattern into the unexpected, from the ordinary into the apocalyptic. The parables seem to speak of familiar things but what happens in the drama which they describe is unknown and unexpected. It proceeds from the new initiative taken by God in and through Christ.

When, after pondering on the parables, one looks back, one can say: what are they in fact about? Composed and told by Christ himself, they come straight from the mind of God and are addressed to human hearts. One can say quite simply: what does God want us to know, what is he saying? The parables tell very little about heaven. They speak, it is true, of the angels quite distinctly and by inference, when they are included among the characters in the stories. Yet the little that is said does not describe the angels' own being and existence but their relationship to human souls. One parable, that of Dives and Lazarus, speaks of the life after death. There again, it does not offer a comprehensive view of the whole. It tells of that portion which the soul meets on the first stage of the heavenly journey, in which the after-effects of the finished life on earth have to be experienced.

To impart knowledge of heaven does not seem to be the purpose of the parables. They are set in this world of earth.

What happens belongs here. They would seem to be intended to instruct those who are here about the meaning of life on earth. The implication is that it is much less the business of people here to get information about heaven than to realise the value of the days and years spent on earth. It can be observed that human souls are variously presented in the stories as labourers, servants and stewards, but never as owners. The ownership of this world is vested in the kingdom of heaven, although the landlord is away at a distance. Great stress is nevertheless laid on the industry and productive capacity of the labourers who work here for the owner. Throughout the parables interest is concentrated not on heaven, but on the earth and the people who dwell there. It is as if God says through these stories, 'You people are on earth but you have not found out why. Now listen.'

Furthermore, the parables are about the earth's history and that of mankind, which is interwoven with it. They are concerned with what has happened and with what happens. Nothing stands still in these stories. They are about people with undertakings. Some are off on journeys, like the prodigal son and the man going from Jerusalem to Jericho. Some have taken on big jobs, like the vine-grower getting in the harvest of grapes, who employs more and more workers as the day lengthens. Others have gone in for commerce and are anxious to make profit. Those on the land are sowing or preparing to reap. Even those with leisure have decided to hold feasts, from the king preparing his son's marriage to Dives, the rich man enjoying life with his brothers. Their happy times were busy ones, in which they carried out their social obligations, even those to the beggar at the gate.

These many undertakings are described as producing change and development. The seed is sown, even if only one quarter bears fruit as it should. The harvest of grapes is gathered, although some labourers complain of their wages. The prodigal son returns home quite changed from the careless youth who left. The man who fell among thieves on the road to Jericho has lost everything and must make a new start. The parables are in reality about man's journey through history from his creation, through the Fall into the influence of evil powers and on into the world-dilemma that ensued. What is thereafter to become of man? He is on earth to take part in history, to make it himself. He has the time, the place and the independence to do it. He should not stand still; he is intended to evolve.

Then again, these stories are about the purpose in the future towards which human history should move. The parables mostly have no true endings. They leave behind a series of open questions. Does the elder brother of the prodigal son take part in the feast of welcome in the end? What became of the man without a wedding garment, of the foolish virgins who bought the oil too late, of the lazy servant who hid the talent? One could say of these stories that they are so much concerned with the future that they cannot end in the present. There is always more to come. The guests are invited but the marriage is to be celebrated beyond the story's end. The bridegroom comes and no more is said because the fulfilment of the expectation is still to come. The treasure is found in the field, the pearl is found and purchased, but for what purpose? It remains to be seen. The Fall of man below that which he was created to be is an assumed fact in the parables. It happened long ago in the past. The drive towards the future is towards overcoming its consequences, towards attaining the Resurrection.

Before the coming of Christ, the religious feeling of good people tended to make them look back in regret to what man had been in his earliest history before the Fall. The trend of events seemed to them to be onwards but downwards at the same time. The stories in the parables present another outlook. The spiritual gaze should be forward-looking. That should be aimed at and achieved which had never been. Man may be fallen but he should rise again. He should strive with energy for resurrection, for the end has not yet come. That should be achieved at the end which will be greater than that which was there in the beginning.

These stories, although they say little of heaven, speak much of God. They show his active interest in human doings on earth and his confidence that something will come of them. The human characters in the parables are not always sure of their purpose. The man without the wedding garment did not know why he had come. The protesting labourers in the vineyard believed that they had done a day's work for the sake of the wages but found themselves in the wrong. The servant who hid the talent missed the point. Some people are shown quite at a loss about the aim of their existence, as indeed others may still be today.

God's confidence in man's purpose shines powerfully by contrast. No uncertainty nor holding back is there to confuse the straight drive towards the future. The initiative is God's in the events of these stories. He sent the sower to sow, the men from the marketplace to work in the vineyard and, from the distance, the servants to collect the produce of the harvest. He, in the form of the king, sent the invitation to the marriage feast. Sent by him, the bridegroom came to meet the wise and foolish virgins. In the guise of the father, he sent the younger son from home, supplied with wealth but without wisdom and welcomed him again on his return. The prime mover in the drama of human history is the kingdom of heaven, intent on humankind coming at the last to the right fulfilment of its purpose. He through whom the divine energy is at work on earth is the Son. He is the sower of the fresh seed. He is the bridegroom, he who comes to bring that to man by which he will have the chance to rise again.

Divine will has been poured, is still poured, into human evolution on earth but not so as to deter the activity of human will. The characters in the stories that are most praised are the ones who show initiative: the treasure-hunter who buys the field, the fisherman who casts the net, and even the dishonest steward who saves himself by cheating. Those who receive the talents and double them are rewarded. The lost son, having wasted his inheritance, receives a welcome unknown before in the father's house, because he has come back by the strength of his own will. Those who undertake things for themselves, who work with a sense of purpose, who are prepared for a new situation, are encouraged and commended in the name of God. He gives strength of will in order to rouse human will, that God and man may work together for the Resurrection. In many of the parables, the one in authority, the lord, calls those under his orders to progress from the outlook of servants to that of fellow workers. They may have started out as stewards and servants but they are expected, if they have an input into what is undertaken, to become partners. In the Old Testament obedience to God was praised as the highest virtue of man. In the New Testament another theme appears in the parables. Man is called upon by God to take his will into his own hands and to act for himself with courage. Man is invited into partnership with God for the making of future history.

Can man be expected to make such an advance? How could he change from obedience to courage, unless he would find some new force within himself? While Christ was telling these stories he was offering from himself a new capacity to human souls, which they had not had earlier. Until then they had been guided by God through the law. The children of Israel believed that their law came directly from Yahweh. All other nations had laws which they held to be divinely inspired. Man-made statutes appeared later in history.

Christ did not deny the law, but he brought what was new, the conscience. It is the voice that speaks from within the single human heart. It is the inner treasure that each one has for himself and yet he knows that each other person possesses it likewise. It is quite individual, but it speaks out of the knowledge of good and evil that comes from God. We know what is good and what is evil because God knows and shares the knowledge with us. The inner sense of right felt in the heart is divine but is treasured by each one as his own. The law spoke for God, the conscience speaks for the human self, but Christ speaks in the conscience of the divine wisdom that is shared with man. The conscience that is true to itself and is not a shadow cast by the influence of public opinion inspires the will to right action. Man can become God's fellow worker because he has wisdom and will of his own to put into the common undertaking. Christ spoke in the parables of the responsibility felt and carried by God for the fulfilment of human evolution. By virtue of the Christ-given conscience man can take his share.

In the parables the storyteller was speaking of himself and of his purpose in coming from the divine world to earth. He was explaining in pictures what scarcely any of his listeners could be expected to understand. The new beginning to world-history had dawned. His hearers were still thinking the old thoughts but they were being offered the new ones. These stories were not only the occasion for teaching people to understand. They were a challenge to the will. They made plain what Christ had come to undertake, with the invitation to take part. The parables are stories to enjoy, but are not for enjoyment. They are to be understood, but are not for understanding. They give motives for action, a purpose to be fulfilled. At the close of the story of the Good Samaritan, Christ asked his listener what it meant. He had grasped the point. He then said to him: 'Go and do likewise.'

This is the ending concealed behind the lack of endings in all the stories: 'Go and do likewise.'